"There are many boo[ks] and they fall into ev[ery category]... crime, romance, science fiction, fantasy, and horror. And if they have the word 'crisis' or 'decline,' they can tip into being self-help, business management, and even home improvement. What I value about this book is that it is theology—as it seeks to address where we are by reminding us of who God is and who we are. Because it puts God in the center, it is a profoundly hope-giving book, engaging us all by diagnosing the real crisis of faith and encouraging us to live alertly and expectantly within that. The church needs teachers like this."

—The Most Rev. Justin Welby, Archbishop of Canterbury

"Andy and Blair have given us a priceless gift. In the midst of ongoing questions about *how* to respond to church decline, they peel back the layers and help us face the deeper questions about *why* we are declining. Resisting the temptation to offer superficial tips and tricks, Andy and Blair invite each faith community and believer to wait and listen for the generative faith God has for each of us and our churches. This book will draw every leader and Jesus follower who wonders what could work today into a deeper, more faith-full relationship with the God who is always working."

—Kara Powell, executive director, Fuller Youth Institute; chief of leadership formation, Fuller Seminary; coauthor of *3 Big Questions That Change Every Teenager*

"There are not many books on what ails the church that I would share with laypeople. This, in fact, might be the only one. Our real crisis—usually misdiagnosed—is that our churches can be great places to hide from God. Root and Bertrand make clear that we must put away our strategies and gimmicks and wait on the Lord all over again. I pray we all would follow this brilliantly antiprogrammatic counsel."

—**Jason Byassee**, senior pastor, Timothy Eaton Memorial
Church, Toronto; coauthor of *Faithful and Fractured:
Responding to the Clergy Health Crisis*

"We're all feeling the crisis of church decline and frantically trying to fix the problem. This groundbreaking book proposes that we've misdiagnosed the problem and that our supposed treatment is actually making things worse. Thankfully, Root and Bertrand offer both a better diagnosis and a helpful, human way forward. Finally, a book that guides the church in practical ways through our actual problem (i.e., trusting in our own action to save the church) to teach us once more to wait upon the God we claim to believe is powerful."

—**Mandy Smith**, pastor and author of *Unfettered: Imagining
a Childlike Faith beyond the Baggage of Western Culture*
and *The Vulnerable Pastor*

"Churches across the West are in decline and, as a result, are trying to do something about it. Andrew Root and Blair Bertrand explain why this is precisely what they should not do. Rather than attempting to whip up a frenzy of programs and activity, Root and Bertrand point churches back to the mystery and power of God, back to waiting on him to do the things that only he can do. Rejecting pithy slogans and slick approaches, this book challenges us to think first about God's place in our church and, in the process, rediscover just how beautiful her life might become once again."

—**Steve Bezner**, senior pastor, Houston Northwest Church

When
Church
Stops
Working

# When Church Stops Working

A Future for Your Congregation beyond
More Money, Programs, and Innovation

Andrew Root and Blair D. Bertrand

BrazosPress

*a division of Baker Publishing Group*
Grand Rapids, Michigan

© 2023 by Andrew Root and Blair Bertrand

Published by Brazos Press
a division of Baker Publishing Group
Grand Rapids, Michigan
www.brazospress.com

Printed in the United States of America

Library of Congress Cataloging-in-Publication Control Number: 2022056551
ISBN 978-1-58743-578-2 (paper)
ISBN 978-1-58743-605-5 (cloth)

Baker Publishing Group publications use paper produced from sustainable forestry practices and post-consumer waste whenever possible.

23   24   25   26   27   28   29       7   6   5   4   3   2   1

To Kenda Creasy Dean,
who showed us how to love the church

# Contents

# Preface

You probably picked up this book because you're concerned about the church and its decline. The good news is that you're in the right place. This book will discuss why the church is in crisis, offering some suggestions for what we can do about it. The bad (or, at least, disorientating) news is that this book will reveal that what you think is the problem isn't really the problem. And the actions you think will help the church may make things worse. This book aims to provide a broader view of the challenges before us, giving us perspective that might keep us from walking in the wrong direction. The book will encourage you to do something, but this something might be more paradoxical than you expect. The point of this book you're holding is to address the church in crisis, but in a way you probably haven't considered.

Since the release of my (Andy's) Ministry in a Secular Age series, I've been getting two kinds of emails. The first type comes from pastors who appreciated those books. They've found that each book names something they had felt but been unable to articulate. After expressing their appreciation for the books, they ask me directly, "But how would you say this all to laypeople, particularly people on church boards or sessions or councils? I mean, it resonates with me, but I don't think my lay leaders can wade through all your cultural philosophy and theology." Good point.

I usually respond by assuring them it can be done. Believing it's possible or calling my bluff, some have been nice enough to invite me to Zoom, or visit in person, with those very boards, sessions, or councils. These pastors basically introduce me to these groups with "This is Andy Root." They then turn to me and say, "Now Andy, tell them all the things about all the stuff." This book will try to do what I do in those presentations: discuss "all the stuff" about our secular age and the challenges the church faces in a way that all who care about these things can understand. Yes, it was hard to limit the footnotes, but you will thank me later.

The second type of email goes something like this: "Dear Professor Root, I've found your books very helpful in naming what's happening and in providing a theological vision. But I'm still stuck on what to do with it all. What steps or actions do I take after reading this? What do my lay leaders and I do next?"

This book is an attempt to respond to these emails as well. It synthesizes the whole Ministry in a Secular Age series in a format aimed at lay leaders. I hope that folks working in sales, IT, education, e-commerce, or not working at all—pretty much any job but pastor or professor—can all read and profit from this book. My aim is to provide a book that pastors can read together with their board, session, or council. The hope is that this little book both serves as a translation of the big ideas from the Ministry in a Secular Age series and provides a kind of map of what small steps can help the church today.

Yet, to be fair, the map doesn't really contain detailed, step-by-step directions. It's surely not a GPS system or even IKEA instructions. There are no six steps or worksheets or inventories (although there is plenty you can discuss with others). If there were, it would go against everything I've described as the crisis we face in the church. Instead of a map, the next steps are a process of being formed, an invitation to find the stories and visions that can lead the church beyond the crisis of decline and into the crisis of an encounter with the living God.

These are big and important questions that I hope you will wrestle with in community. Read this book with others, together leaning into what it means for your congregation and ministry. There are big ideas in this little book, but also a lot of handles that will help your church and ministry. There are no quick fixes. As a matter of fact, the very assumption of a quick fix misinforms and malforms the church and the church's leaders.

I keep saying "I" because this book is the offspring of the six other books from that series I've authored. But I haven't written this little book alone. If you read through the preface of those six other volumes (though why would you unless you're a major preface nerd?), you'll see that in each one I thank Blair Bertrand, whom I've known for twenty years. We met next to a dumpster at Princeton Theology Seminary, an ominous place to start a friendship. That friendship quickly shifted to the hockey rink, but we forged our friendship around theological ideas more than around men's league hockey. Blair has been reading my work and providing some of the best engagement with it for two decades. He read some of my earliest seminary papers and every book since. No one understands my project more than Blair. This is true in part because Blair's own project has similar points of emphasis. Blair is one of the best, most insightful readers I know. But he is more than that. He is a wonderful teacher, able to take the most complex ideas and translate them for laypeople. Blair has led several church councils and sessions in the same way we hope this book will lead you. Blair comes to this task as a skilled scholar and seasoned pastor. It made all sorts of sense for me to invite Blair to coauthor this book with me.

To begin our thanks, I want to first thank Blair both for his friendship and for his help in shaping this book for you, the reader. The origins of this book go back to Bob Hosack. In the academic world, people talk about their Herr Professor, using the formal German title as a sign of deep respect. If there is such a thing as a Herr Editor, for me it's Bob. Bob had the vision for the Ministry in a Secular Age series and for this book too. After hearing that the Lilly Endowment was investing in a project to work out the implications of the Ministry in a Secular Age series, Bob suggested the book you're holding. I want to thank Bob for all he has done for me. And I want to thank the Eli Lilly Endowment, particularly Jessicah Duckworth, Chanon Ross, and Chris Coble, for funding a grant called Relevance to Resonance. I've worked on that grant (and many others) with my dear friend David Wood. David's impact on American Protestantism is immense. He has mentored and shaped so many pastors in the church. Watching him do that directly through our grants has been a marvelous experience. As always, I want to thank Kara Root for her faithful reading and editing of my chapters in this project, like all others.

Both Blair and I would also like to thank Eric Salo for his superb editing work. We appreciate that he was gentle when he killed all the footnotes. We'd also like to thank Kenda Creasy Dean, to whom this book is dedicated. Her scholarship has always been done in loving service to the church. She insists that the Holy Spirit doesn't just live in ivory towers but is on the loose in the world. For book nerds like us, her insistence that ideas make a difference in the world only when the world can understand them has been a challenge and an inspiration.

I (Blair) want to thank Andy. There is an African proverb that says, "If you want to go fast, go alone. If you want to go far, go together." Anyone who knows Andy knows that he works fast. People often wonder if he ever sleeps, because it seems like he always has a new book coming out (for the record, he does). He most often works alone, going fast. To partner on this project was a risk for him. He had to go forward together, a bit slower but in the end, I hope, a bit farther than he might have done alone. I also want to thank the elders and lay leaders I have had the honor of working with over the years. My thanks go to Debi Chadsey and Debbie Jones, who took a chance to hire me the first time, to passionate denominational leaders like Jo Morris and Jen DeCombe, and to visionary elders like Jim Christian and Rod Thomson. There are so many more folks who have kept it real, skewering any pretension I might have, and who have led the church forward into a hopeful and faithful future. The first lay leader who shaped me was my mom, Sheryl Bertrand. Singing in the choir, organizing the women's ministry, chairing the church council, my mom has done it all. She has always shown me that the church is an imperfect but good community where we might encounter each other and God. Any errors that remain in the book are Andy's (and, I guess, mine), but the strengths come from the questions and efforts of a host of lay leaders we have been privileged to work with. Thanks.

# 1

# Why Your Church Has a Problem, but It Isn't What You Think

## Church in Crisis: Influence, People, and Belief

"Make America Great Again." No matter who you are in today's America, these are fighting words. Some believe the decline of the US is real: they want to return to a great past. Others scoff that America was never great: they strive for a better tomorrow. The irony of the slogan is that it spurs everybody into political action but for different reasons, some based on a wistful sense of the past, others based on dreams of a better future. At their best, conservatives want to recapture the greatest parts of yesterday, while liberals strive to build progressively toward a better future.

Sometimes we lose the fact that both groups, conservatives and liberals, don't like the current situation. Conservatives look around and see decline, while liberals point to dreams deferred. The present gets measured against a golden past or a perfect future. How can the present measure up when the criterion is always something we imagine, not something real? Sure, both the past and the future are "real," but the funny thing about time is that we cannot live in either the past or the future. We can tell ourselves stories of the glory days and we can imagine tales of what might come, but we can't actually be in the past or the future.

This is true of the church just as much as it is true of America. "Make First Church of Somewhere Great Again" prompts gut feelings in First Church's leaders. Conservatives wring their hands about how the church has declined. Liberals fret that the church will never reach its full potential to transform society. There is a feeling of not enough: too little influence, too few people, too fragile belief. Conservatives try to recapture something lost, and liberals marshal the right changes to make a difference. While both sides might differ in approach, recovering or reimagining, what they hold in common is that both believe the church does not have enough at the moment. The answer to the problem of not enough is *more*, regardless of tactic.

This dynamic plays out in the polarized culture wars that rage in very public settings. On one side there are battles over prayer in schools or the Ten Commandments in courthouses, attempts to influence public piety and morality. On the other side there are fights for racial justice and advocacy for marginalized groups, efforts to influence the future of society toward the common good. At the root, these are fights over the proper separation of church and state.[1] There is a formal division: legally there is no state religion, but materially the church still plays a role in the life of the people. The culture wars provide an obvious example, but there are many ways that the church tries to insert itself into the public conversation. There is some sense that in the past, the church was the moral conscience of the nation, or that the church should act prophetically and call the nation to account for its actions.

COVID-19 only sharpened the blending of religion and public life. Some, in the name of Christian freedom, rejected public health orders about masking or gathering. Others, in the name of Christian charity, advocated for lockdowns and vaccinations. Even if First Church of Somewhere is not particularly conservative or liberal, is not a declared soldier in the culture war, its leaders had to decide how the community would navigate their Christian commitments in relation to public health mandates. Whatever the case, the church had to relate with public health policies, recapturing or creating its status as the moral conscience of the nation-state.

In the wake of the pandemic, First Church of Somewhere wrestles with questions of fewer people. There is a minor industry analyzing the demographics of church attendance, and there is no shortage of material. Even the idea of church attendance is up for debate. What should we measure? Besides worship attendance, we could look at dollars going to community ministry, number of church users per week, or how many hits (and for how long) our online content generates. Most church consultants say you need to pick the right metrics and continually measure them to know your church's health. But choosing which metric is dizzying and far more complicated than a leader at First Church of Somewhere can expect to understand.

Despite all of this analysis, the motivation to measure is the same: How can we get more people? When leaders sit in a meeting to discuss budget and worship and the future, some

3

remember days of yore when the church was bursting at the seams. Others look at the local megachurch with envy and wonder why people would flock there. (And not here! Our theology is better!) At no point does anyone ever suggest that First Church of Somewhere has enough people; all of them know the solution: more people.

In the quest for more people, the leaders of First Church of Somewhere face a choice. Either they must define belief narrowly so that those who hold that belief will find them attractive, or they must pitch a big tent in terms of belief to capture the many ways that people find meaning. The first strategy resembles that of a restaurant that has one thing on the menu (pizza, burgers, shawarma, etc.). The second place has a huge menu with a bit of everything. If you've ever had to choose a restaurant for a group, you know that the narrow menu can put some off, but the large menu makes no one happy.

Realistically, the leaders of First Church of Somewhere might realize that it takes a lot of resources to offer a large menu of programs and activities. If they are a small church with little money, they might double down on some of their core beliefs and pitch a kind of niche church experience. Once they have taken that approach for a while and have gathered resources, they could introduce another program or activity. As they expand, they will need to stay true to their mission and their core beliefs, which is hard because new programs bring different people who make meaning in different ways. Large churches face the problem of unity (a common set of beliefs) within diversity (different ways of making meaning). Push unity of beliefs too much and you exclude those who don't hold those beliefs. Emphasize diversity too much and you introduce conflict and apathy because people either defend their beliefs or don't care enough to take part.

4

## A Terminal Diagnosis

Like many, the leaders at First Church of Somewhere believe they know the problem in the church: too little influence, too few people, too fragile belief. We see this in their constant search for more resources and more relevance. The lack of resources and relevance pains leaders, making them anxious and stressed. Some feel this pain acutely because they have some sense that the church had more resources and relevance in the not too distant past. It is more painful to lose something than to never know what you are missing. Others pine for a better future, promised but not attainable. Nostalgia and hope are powerful emotions that, in this case, both lead to pain.

Adding to the problem is the fact that the church is in a vicious circle. If we had more resources, we could be more relevant, but we can't be more relevant without more resources. Church leaders feel the loss and vicious circle in their gut, and so they understandably look for a way out.

Luckily for them, just as many people who recognize the problem have a solution. The cure is to be more effective and therefore increase resources while using them efficiently. Coupled with effectiveness is a drive for innovation. How many times have we heard that we must creatively meet the needs of the surrounding community? The solution is the right balance of resource management and effective innovation, which makes our church grow sustainably.

Church leaders can choose one of two aids in their search for effective innovation, both of which offer simple instructions. The first approach attempts to learn how successful churches have become more effective and innovative. They essentially say, "We did it this way and so, if you want to be successful like us, don't reinvent the wheel, just do it exactly as we did." They offer a very clear and can't-miss, ready-made template for a church to fit into. The second approach offers a set process that any church can use to make its own decisions about how to innovate effectively. It recognizes that each church is different (so one template doesn't fit) but think that there is an underlying process that applies to all congregations. The outcomes differ from church to church, but how the two approaches go about doing it is the same. The first gives you a recipe; the second gives you some general cooking guidelines. In either case, you end up with a perfectly baked church.

As a leader, your job is to find the right recipe or the right process for your church. While writing this book, we combed our libraries for resources that give you just the right advice. Why reinvent the wheel? We noticed something strange. As we read, all of those books—whether published in the 1970s, '80s, '90s, '00s, or in a post-COVID world—sounded the same and gave the same advice: effective innovation. Fifty years separates our oldest church health book and the most recent. We point this out not to make fun of 2020 or to disparage 1970. Rather, we point it out because if the solution to the church's problem has remained the same for fifty years, then one of two things is true. The problem is wicked, meaning there is no actual solution, in which case we need to despair. Or those books misdiagnose the problem. Effective innovation has failed to solve the problem of too little influence, too few people, too fragile belief, not because of a problem with the solution but because those books are trying to solve the wrong problem.

We agree with those who say that there is a problem in the church today. We just don't agree with them that the problem is too little influence, too few people, too fragile belief. Much of the North American church is facing a crisis. Our read of the situation is that the lack of influence, people, and belief is a symptom, not a problem. When we pull back and look at some larger issues going on in the world, we see a different diagnosis of the problem, and therefore we prescribe a different cure. Effective innovation has not stopped the crisis in the church because the crisis comes from the very place that effective innovation comes from: the secular age. Instead of helping the church, effective innovation actually worsens the crisis by driving us deeper into the secular age we find ourselves in.

Before diving into how effective innovation is a key part of the secular age and therefore a big part of our problem as the church, stop for a moment and think about your own health. Pretend you have some obvious symptoms, like a sore stomach, but you do not know why you have the pain. Understandably, you want to feel healthy. Your life isn't as good when you are in pain and worried about it. In theory, we know that without the right diagnosis, we can't get the correct treatment. In reality, we aren't always so open.

This truth, that we want a diagnosis because we want to get rid of the pain but we aren't patient with the long process of finding out the reality, becomes clear when someone we love goes to the emergency room. We want answers now! Just tell us what's wrong so we can do something about it. Never mind the fact that doctors spend years learning how to tease apart different symptoms to discover the underlying cause. We can see the symptoms, and a few Google searches later we know the cause. Waiting for doctors to confirm our diagnosis frustrates us, especially because many times, a commonsense diagnosis prevails. A patient's kidneys are shutting down, so the kidney specialist is called in. The doctor asks questions, runs tests, and confidently prescribes treatment. The patient recovers, returning to normal life with a story to tell. Probing beyond symptoms to causes has resulted in a match, which even Google predicted, between diagnosis and the correct treatment.

But more times than we would like to admit, common sense leads us astray. A patient's kidneys are shutting down, so it must be a problem with the kidneys, right? Except it isn't. Rare, like one-in-a-million rare, autoimmune blood conditions can affect kidney functioning. In that case, the patient needs a blood specialist, not a kidney specialist. The kidneys are a symptom, but the diagnosis reveals they aren't the problem. Treat the kidneys and the patient will die because the real problem will continue. It is in these cases that Google really fails and angers doctors. The patient is convinced that they know both the symptoms and the correct diagnosis for those symptoms. "Just give me the cure that I already know," they say. Common sense confuses our symptoms with the true reason for why we feel the way we do.

Some of our hardest times are when we go to the doctor expecting a simple, commonsense diagnosis only to receive terrible news. Your stomach has been hurting for a while, so you think it's probably an ulcer (Google says so and your Uncle Ralph had one, so it makes sense). A day later, the doctor's office calls and tells you to come in because they found something more serious—cancer. Your normal life gets thrown into chaos, made worse because you always feel like you are waiting. Waiting to find out how bad it is. Waiting for a clear diagnosis. Waiting for a spot to open up. Waiting for the results of a test. Waiting for normal life to resume. There is nothing fast about cancer treatment, made all the worse by the impending sense that death is much closer than it was before the diagnosis.

We are both doctors, albeit not medical doctors. We have spent years studying the church, honing our diagnostic skills and coming up with prescriptions that can lead to health. You might want to sit down for this. Let's start with the bad news. Your church is sick. But that isn't the worst part of it. We believe that someone has misdiagnosed it. The treatment plan commonly prescribed—effective innovation—will only cause your church to remain sick.

The good news is that your church can get healthy, though it won't be easy. The first challenge is to change your mindset: Your church is sick, but the problem is not decline. The problem is that the secular age has infected it. When someone, or in this case something, gets sick because of a larger, systemic cause, the complexity of the treatment ramps up. Focusing on the sick individual will only get you so far if the surrounding air is poisoned. Like helping fish in polluted water, we can't just treat the fish. We need to treat the pollution, which is a much bigger task.

## The Secular Age in Three Parts

All of this may seem abstract, so let's start with three clear signs of decline that most churches experience. Symptom 1 of the secular age is a sense that the church and Christianity have less influence in society than they once did. Mainline denominations sending letters to government officials decrying various justice issues is a residual form of the moral power the church once wielded. Or a pastor attending a city council meeting to give their opinion about some legislation. Do elected representatives really care about what churches and pastors think? Usually no, because they don't count for many votes. Churches believe that the nation and the church once shared a common morality. The politicians less so. For many Christians, the prophetic task of the church is to hold the state accountable, a job that is possible only if the church and the state share the same sense of justice. Any time we hear calls about returning to the Christian foundations of the nation-state, we are hearing symptom 1.

The cause of symptom 1 is that the sacred no longer sets the agenda for all of society. For example, our justice system no longer assumes a Christian foundation. The law against murder remains and has good reasons behind it even if society does not believe that the Ten Commandments are God's law. Other faiths prohibit murder without needing to rely on Moses and the stone tablets. Secular humanists forbid murder based on an understanding of human rights that makes no appeal to faith. Society agrees that murder is bad, though we have different reasons for believing that. Justice becomes what we can agree on regardless of our beliefs and practices. Appeals to "what the Bible says" don't hold up in court because we do not recognize the sacred as an authority for all of society. It makes sense, then, that if our public lives don't share the same foundation, then the church's influence over society can spread only as much as it can convince everyone else that it is right. The culture wars stem in part from attempts by Christians to build a moral majority or a campaign to advance their vision of the ideal society.

Symptom 2 follows from this. Whereas symptom 1 divides the sacred and the secular, leading to less influence, symptom 2 divides the public and the private, leading to fewer people in churches. Survey after survey tells us what we already know—fewer people are going to church. Those reports and surveys tell us about the rise of the "nones," people who respond "none" to the question "What religion do you identify with?" Even before the rise of the nones, there had been ongoing attrition, with each generation attending church less often than the one before. Fewer people express their faith in public ways. That doesn't mean that people don't have a faith or that people don't express that faith. But that faith has become private, not public.

Fewer people at church does not mean less belief, just like going to church doesn't mean you are super faithful. What it means, though, is that the connection between our personal beliefs and public expression does not line up with how it once was in the past.

Fewer people, symptom 2, stems from a divide between the public and the private. If our society can go along just fine without a sacred foundation—murder is still murder, whether or not I believe in the Ten Commandments—it becomes optional for me to take part in religion. My motivation for going to church changes from participation in a public profession of faith to participation in a private experience. Perhaps I go because I have strong personal beliefs about a moral cause (think abortion) or how society should be (think Black Lives Matter), and the church can help with that. Or maybe it is simply that I want my kids to live good, moral lives. There continues to be some vague sense that the church is the place where our children can learn how to be good. In that case, I go to church for the sake of my children, unless there is something else that would be better for my kids, such as travel soccer or visiting family for the weekend. I go to church if I get something out of it, but I don't go for anyone else. My personal beliefs don't connect to public expressions in powerful ways.

Now we come to symptom 3, which is the sense that belief itself has changed. The decline of denominations coupled with the explosion of nondenominational churches points to the fact that people have a very wide range of beliefs. At one point, if you were a Presbyterian or a Lutheran or a Methodist, it meant that you believed certain things about God. There might have been differences of belief between denominations that played out in how they organized and worshiped. But now you can walk into two churches from the same denomination

11

and you might think they have nothing in common. Or you can walk into a nondenominational church that holds to a very general understanding of God captured in their relatively simple faith statement. Because our society has split the sacred and the secular, the public and the private, people hold a wide assortment of beliefs about God. For the first time in history, it is possible that they can even not believe in God at all. We no longer believe a person needs to change their personal beliefs to fit public expression; we believe that the public expression should change to match the personal beliefs of everyone.

Symptom 3 goes deep to the core—it is now possible to not believe in God. The idea that a person could believe there is no God goes beyond simple atheism. Here, the divide occurs between the immanent and the transcendent. "Immanent" simply means those things that we can see around us, stuff that we can measure, objects that we can track and see their cause and effect. Immanent thinking gives us modern medicine and engineering because we can harness and control the natural processes of the world for our own ends. We understand illness to be the result of a virus, not some kind of spiritual punishment. The opposite of immanent is transcendent, meaning those things that are beyond our perception, above our ability to control and determine, even in some ways objects that are supernatural, that defy explanation. In most places and in most times, people have assumed that the world is larger than just what we can see, measure, and control. Humans normally assumed that there was a spiritual world and that it could interact with our material world. Sociologists sometimes call this an "enchanted" world, because the immanent and the transcendent permeate each other. It is now possible to not believe that, something unique to our time.

## The Secular Imagination

Combining these three divisions—secular and sacred, public and private, immanent and transcendent—gives us the secular age we live in. Churches can try to solve the common problems of influence, attendance, and belief, but they are up against cultural forces much larger than the individual problems seem to suggest. Let's be clear, we do not believe that the cure for the secular age is some kind of new sacred age. That ship has sailed. Nor do we hold out much hope for the strategies used to combat these problems, because they find their inspiration within the secular age. We end up trying to win a game playing by rules that are stacked against us when we should instead reimagine the game itself.

In this book, we want to reimagine the church within the secular age. We believe God continues to act in the world, and because God acts in the world, we believe it is possible for the church to flourish. The first part of our diagnosis is that the problem the church faces today is that the symptoms don't follow common sense but are part of a larger problem we call the secular age, and the second part is that we miss that fact because the secular age has captured our imaginations. The sickness in the church fools us by hiding as the cure, a fact that we can't see because it was a slow trip to get here. If you want a healthy church, you are going to need to imagine a cure that doesn't depend on the secular age.

This talk of imagination can seem vague to those of us used to working in the real world. After all, imagination is the domain of artists, poets, and theologians, not carpenters, engineers, and accountants. Don't even mention imagination to those scientists dedicated to the cold, hard facts. For someone really invested in the literal or concrete, reality appears to be a given that does not require imagination for us to use or understand. We disagree. Even people committed to a concrete or literal understanding of the world still use imagination all the time. Carpenters and biologists might imagine different futures for a stand of trees. One sees furniture and houses, while the other sees bioremediation or wildlife habitat. Neither actually "sees" these things, but they sense the possibilities inherent in the forest, possibilities shaped by their experiences and understandings of how and why the world works. It is that sense, that understanding of what this reality is and could be, that is at the heart of imagination. The trees are no less real or concrete whether a carpenter or naturalist looks at them, but their different imaginations open up different parts of that reality.

Because the secular age separates the secular and the sacred, making belief private and the immanent the agreed-upon public reality, the church has a hard time imagining what a public faith that witnesses to the transcendent looks like. Our imaginations are secular, so when we try to imagine the sacred, try to see God at work in our lives and in the world, we can do so only in secular terms. The problem is so deep that even when we experience something meaningful, something sacred and transcendent, the only language we have to describe it is secular. It is as if we have looked at the world with a secular lens for so long that when something sacred appears, we can't see it for what it is, nor do we even have the language to describe it. Consider the carpenter and the biologist again. They both imagine a different goal, something they are working toward. One sees well-built houses filled with cheerful people, the other a natural habitat that is self-sustaining and healthy. Both are good. Who doesn't want to live in a delightful house and have a beautiful environment? But we can't have both. If the carpenter cuts down the trees, the biologist's dream ends, and vice versa. How can we make a decision if we do not have the ability or language to see what the other wants or sees? How can we choose whose imagined future is best?

## The Secular Imagination: Acceleration versus Resonance

This choice between imagined futures plays out even more forcefully in our personal lives. In our limited lifetime we have to make choices to pursue some things and, because we are pursuing those things, leave others behind. We obsess over work-life balance, making sure that we give sufficient time to our various roles. Both of us want to be a good son, brother, husband, father, friend, academic, and hockey player, all while staying on top of reality TV, the latest music, our fantasy football pool, walking the dog, and doing the dishes. Each of those roles and desires makes demands on our limited time, so we must choose what we will do and not do. Efficiency is often the solution. We double up, listening to a podcast for work while we walk the dog. We think we can do more than we actually can, and we say things like, "After we write this book, life will calm down." Except it never does. Add to this that each of those roles means that we have to decide about other people's time, "Am I going to drive to this practice or play a game with this kid or help my aging parents with their yard work?" You see just how big the problem is. We need more time.

Here is where secular logic takes over. We have no way of knowing what task is valuable or how much is enough. The only thing we know is that we need good things and more of them. The busyness we experience comes from the feeling that we need to accelerate every part of our lives. Sometimes we notice this acceleration. We go on vacations where we pack so much in that it feels like an extension of our everyday life. When we have to-do lists for our time off, is it really time off? Or we are so busy we cannot take a vacation. Or we hit a wall, have a heart attack, or stress causes our body to just stop. Secular logic tells us that there are two speeds—fast or dead. We can try to slow down, but we still feel the pull either to speed up or to give up. The secular age accelerates our lives, and we can only imagine more or nothing.

Our diagnosis is that the opposite of acceleration isn't dead or slow. The opposite of more is resonance. Resonance is an experience of fullness, of being in sync, of being so present to someone or something else that we feel like we have discovered ourselves again. We can resonate with something whether we are moving fast or slow. Often resonance is timeless. We look up at the clock and wonder how it got to be that time because we were so engaged in whatever we were doing that time became irrelevant. Or the moment is so full, so powerful, that something that takes seconds feels much longer. Resonance is all about connecting with the world, with the people in our lives, and finding a meaning that is greater than what we can see and explain. Resonance is about the sacred, the public, and the transcendent.

## Resonance at Work and Love

Again, the carpenters and biologists who are reading this, those who love the concrete and literal, are wondering what the heck we are talking about. Resonance can seem fuzzy. That's part of the point. When we don't have the imagination for something, we can't really see it clearly, and when we can't see it clearly, we can't talk about it well. We can't imagine resonance because the secular age blinds us, and so we lack the vision and language to talk about it. But just because we can't see resonance clearly doesn't mean that we can't see it at all.

Many of us, most of us actually, including the carpenters and biologists, have some sense that there are moments in our lives that are more amazing than others. Often these moments come in a relationship or when we are doing something very meaningful. These moments rise above our everyday lives. They shape who we are and how we relate to the world. These moments surprise us with their power. They come to us just when we need them or force us to change in unexpected ways. Often these moments give us a sense of purpose and meaning that is difficult to articulate but that we know at some deep level is true and right and good. They set us on a meaningful trajectory.

Talking about these things is hard. We've gone to plenty of funerals where the eulogy for the deceased is simply an itinerary of their lives. Person X was born here, married this person, worked here, had this hobby, and now has died. Is life really just an accumulation of events? We don't think so. Times and places sometimes carry more weight than stops along the way. Who hasn't gone back to a place that seems very common to anyone else but is extraordinary to you because of what happened there? Relationships are not just facts; there are deeper qualities to them that make them rich and important. Life must have resonance; otherwise it is just busyness.

If the church needs more of anything in the crisis it faces, it is more resonance. More resonance will bring about deeper relationships and a clearer purpose. Instead of searching for more influence, we will experience deeper connection to God and each other. The crisis of fewer people in the church will fade because we will know how to have relationships that give us a full life. Questions about belief will shift from privately held dogmas to open discussions about God's actions in my life.

Earlier, we asked you to sit down to get the bad news. We live in a secular age, one that divides the sacred from the secular,

17

the public from the private, and the transcendent from the immanent. The secular age hides itself from us because we can only imagine the world in secular, private, and immanent terms. Our lives get busy, our relationships get strained, and our work gets difficult. This goes for our personal lives as well as the life of our church. We try solutions and try solutions and try solutions, usually by being more efficient and innovative, and yet we never seem to have enough influence, people, or belief.

Yet, there is some good news. The church has been here before. The first church faced uncertainty about how it should relate to the world around it. A few disciples huddled in a locked room were definitely no powerhouse in terms of resources. Even with all the teachings of Jesus, most early Christians didn't really know what to make of his life, death, and resurrection.

And what did Jesus tell them to do? Go and effectively innovate? Nope. He told them to wait. That is where we turn in the next chapter.

# 2

# Busy People, Busy Church— A Killer Cocktail

## Get Busy and Wait

Superhero movies are huge right now. Some people, such as Martin Scorsese, deride them. Many people love them; otherwise studios wouldn't keep pumping them out. They are huge not just in their over-the-top CGI effects and grandiosity (yet again the universe is in danger!) but also in the sheer number of details that connect them all together. The story arc of any given hero extends beyond one movie. There are prequels, sequels, appearances in other heroes' movies, and ensemble pieces, not to mention the reboots. The casual viewer has a hard time keeping all the details straight. More than once our kids have reminded us of some detail buried deep in the first movie that only becomes important in what feels like the sixteenth.

With these long character arcs and the serial nature of story-telling on TV, where each episode builds on the last, we seem to have a need for an origin story. Where does it all begin? What is it that sets the hero on this journey? Why does the action develop in this way? Who are the important people in the hero's life? All of these questions find their answer in a good origin story. It is almost like if you get the origin story right, the rest of the movies write themselves.

Like every superhero, your church has an origin story. There are events and people who shaped your congregation into existence. Perhaps the story doesn't have the same drama as Batman or Black Widow, but you tell it anyway, sometimes on Founder's Day or Anniversary Sunday and sometimes in elder meetings or when you are searching for a new pastor. We tell the story of our beginnings because, no matter the hardships we faced, we emerged victorious. At one point we didn't exist, and now we do! Success!

For a while it seemed as if every successful church's backstory started in the Acts of the Apostles. Bill Hybels tells of giving up a bright future as a businessman to start an Acts 2 kind of church. Willow Creek Community Church became the largest church in North America. Success! Rick Warren defied conventional wisdom by planting Saddleback Community Church in a rented theater in Orange County. By following the principles laid out in Acts 2, it has become a multinational, multi-site church. Success! In case you think it is only boomers who have had success, GenXer Mark Driscoll planted Mars Hill, a Seattle church that had over fifteen thousand in attendance at its peak. Success! The church-planting network that grew out of that ministry called itself Acts 29, a not subtle reminder that even though the book ends at chapter 28, we are to live into God's kingdom.

These are all megachurch examples for a reason. North American think that more is better, and that means mega is better than micro. The First Church of Nowhere doesn't offer summits, associations, or networks, because no one wants to hear from a church that can barely sustain itself. Small church leaders attend conferences to hear megachurch pastors tell them how to get more for their small church. Although being mega doesn't mean "too big to fail" (exhibit A: Mars Hill; more on that later), being micro does mean that existence is tenuous. No one wants to make the Christmas appeal just to meet the annual budget (and pastor's salary) for the year. Small churches strive for more people, more resources, and more influence because the alternative to more isn't less. It's death.

Big and small churches, mega and micro, can look at Acts 2:46–47 as a desirable origin story:

> Day by day, as they spent much time together in the temple, they broke bread at home and ate their food with glad and generous hearts, praising God and having the goodwill of all the people. And day by day the Lord added to their number those who were being saved.

Getting together for worship and having fellowship should lead to more people. More, even just a little more, is better.

The real story of the beginning of the church doesn't start in Acts 2, however. Origin stories have a certain inevitability to them. We don't have origin stories for heroes who don't make it. It is inevitable that they will triumph. This triumphalism fits well with the secular story we live in: more is better. In this telling, Acts is a story of progress. The church starts small and gets big. The church starts in one place and moves to many places. Progress is the story of more, the opposite of decline. We don't want to hear the story of church plants failing, congregations closing and selling their buildings, denominations letting go of staff, budgets not getting met. There is no decline, at least from the perspective of the secular age, because that story does not get told. We focus on Pentecost and the idealized community that results, because the way we see it, the megachurch was the inevitable result of that story.

What we don't want to admit is that the real church started out scared and uncertain. Threatened from the outside by those who said the church was wrong about who Jesus was and betrayed from within by its very own leaders, triumph and progress were far from certain. The truth is, Acts 2:46–47 never happened in a widespread manner. The evidence from other parts of the Bible and from what we can reconstruct of early Christians is that the early church struggled mightily. Acts 2 was an aspiration, a goal, a dream. We dream of triumph from a place of defeat, hope from despair. The secular age and its insistence on progress, more, and triumph prevent us from seeing that in fact the church started in a much different way.

The books of the Bible didn't come to us with titles. At some point, we made them up. Strangely enough, we called this book the "Acts of the Apostles." Though that name was assigned long before the secular age, it perfectly encapsulates one of the deeper problems we see with the secular age: it focuses on human action and loses any sense of divine action.[1] This is the temptation of the immanent frame, and it's how Hybels, Warren, and Driscoll approach the text. True, the book recounts human action directed to God, but that is not its main point. The main point is God's action directed to humans. If we read the story, we realize the name really should be the "Acts of God."

Within the first sentences of Acts we hear about Jesus, the Holy Spirit, and God. Luke, the author of both the Gospel of

Luke and the book of Acts, starts with what God has done in Jesus and the Holy Spirit. The first five verses are all God. Jesus acts, teaches, presents himself alive, appears, and speaks about the kingdom of God. God raises Jesus to heaven, gives instructions through the Holy Spirit, and chooses apostles. The Holy Spirit helps God instruct and is the promise of God, coming in baptism upon the disciples. All this happens in five verses!

In Acts 1:4 we read that the first command Jesus gives the disciples is "not to leave Jerusalem." We might have expected that first command to be to go out, to witness, to start a program, to preach, to teach, to do something, anything, that would make the church bigger. But Jesus orders the disciples to stay in Jerusalem and wait. The real origin story of the church does not start in Acts 2 with progress and growth. The real origin story starts in Acts 1 with waiting for God to act. God is the hero, and the church waits.

We've found that when we talk about the church starting with waiting, we receive a lot of pushback. Waiting meets none of our criteria for success, because more waiting feels like more of nothing. We are used to the idea that what we do makes a difference, so when push comes to shove, we resist the idea that waiting for God is the place to start. The more theologically sophisticated folks will throw the word "quietism" at us. Quietism is a heresy, a form of Christian mysticism that gets rid of all human will so that God's will is everything. It avoids doing something so that God can, which sounds pious but usually looks like long sessions of prayer that don't result in any action. Let's be clear: neither the early church nor we are quietists. Waiting, as practiced by the disciples and advocated by us, is not inactive. It is responsive. God acts and we respond. What we are saying, though, is that the secular age blinds us to God's action, and so all we are left with is our action.

There is another response to the idea that the church starts in waiting. The secular age blinds us to God's action, but, even further, it makes the very possibility of God's action impossible to imagine. We hear the promise of Acts 1, that God has done all of these things, and in our heart of hearts we think, "Really?" We have no way of imagining what it would look like for God to act in our lives. What does God look like? Sound like? Act like? In the secular age we can easily imagine religion. We can think of rules and ethics, traditions and practices, because these are *human* actions. But it is much more difficult to imagine that we have those things only because God has already acted in the world. In the end, perhaps our greatest fear is that we will wait, but God will not show up. This is faith: that what God has promised, God will do. This is hope: that the God who began a good work will see it to completion.

If we are to take our own origin story seriously, we need to see that God's people only ever act in response to God's act. They do not plan their own activity and then proceed. They encounter God and act in obedience to that encounter. God acts through God's people, not in the way a puppet master manipulates a marionette but in the manner of a relationship that starts with God's action.

### George and the Acceleration of Society

If we wait on God so that we can act in response, it is important that we can see and hear God. Without first seeing and hearing God, our actions are just *our* actions, not a response. But who has time for that kind of waiting? George does.

In days gone past, people with Down syndrome lived in group homes and had day programs to keep them busy. George was one such person. Even though he was an adult, George had never lived on his own. He was always surrounded by other residents and care workers. The joker in the group, George laughed like a braying donkey. Everyone knew when George was in the house, and everyone loved it. Each day, he would go off to a program, often centered on some sort of simple craft, producing various things that only a mother could appreciate. But George's mother had died some years ago, so he made his crafts for no one in particular. It was the very definition of busywork: he was busy producing something to get some kind of recognition, but he never fulfilled that goal.

At some point the leaders of this program recognized that making paper angels day after day was not a meaningful way to spend a life, no matter who it was. In their way, they loved George and wanted him to have some fulfillment. They searched out and found a small local business that needed repetitive and simple tasks of the kind that George excelled at. Instead of making crafts, George was now making small wooden boxes to hold artisan jams and jellies. The social benefit to George was deemed enough payment, so he was paid much less than another worker would receive. This assumption might actually have been true, though unjust. George was genuinely happy and would go to work with a spring in his step.

The economics of not paying George a full salary worked well for the company. Their product was more attractive but not more expensive. Sales increased. So did the demand for the small wooden boxes. Soon the demand was too much for George to keep up with. Instead of going a few mornings a week, he had to go every morning. Then afternoons. Then full days. Then Monday to Friday, nine to five. His time was getting eaten up by work. He started to feel it. There was less spring in his step and less laughing and more mistakes and complaining.

Finally, George was fired. He was too slow to be productive. He couldn't keep up.

This story has multiple levels of potential blame. Perhaps the jams and jellies company could be blamed for exploiting George. They benefited from him working for less money than someone else might have. Within capitalism, that's just savvy business. We only have a sense of injustice when we compare how George gets treated with how a "normal" person is treated. George does an equally good job, but he isn't as fast. Capitalism works by going fast. The one who works the fastest is the best and therefore worth more. Those, like George, who are slow are not as good and therefore worth less. If we were to make the company pay George the same as someone else, he would get fired because his time is not as worthwhile as someone else's.

It's hard to blame the company for playing by the rules of capitalism. There are more or less ethical ways to be a capitalist, but in North America everyone plays by capitalism's rules. One of those rules is "time is money." In the ideal world, the more you can do in a given unit of time, the more money you can make. In George's case, the more boxes you can make in an hour, the more your salary will be. As a society we make laws to put checks on this rule. For instance, there are supposed to be limits on how many hours someone can work. And companies can't employ children. These limits prove the rule that time is money, pushing us to go faster and faster.

Perhaps the blame for the situation lies on the caregivers. They act as George's guardians and want what is best for him. From their viewpoint, doing crafts is not as fulfilling as making something to sell. Hard to argue against that. Any parent who has had to fake enthusiasm about a preschool art project knows that not all creations are equal. In the ideal world, crafts lead to something else, to an ability to make something useful to the world. The activity of making the craft, say paper angels, is not valuable in itself. The value it has comes from where it might lead. Take LEGO as another example. We expect a child to make bridges out of LEGO bricks, but if they continue to do that into adulthood, we count it a waste. LEGO building should lead to engineering or something helpful to society. George had mastered paper angels, so he was ready for the real activity of making something that could be sold.

What if paper angels or LEGO bridges are just fine as activities in themselves? Sometimes we nod in this direction when we applaud a person's hobbies. Craft stores and complicated LEGO sets aren't strictly for kids. The rule, though, is that a hobby is something that we do in addition to our real, meaningful activity. A few exceptional individuals can elevate their paper angels or LEGO bridges to art. Go on YouTube and you'll find that they are no longer hobbyists but professionals. Similar to how we measure the value of our time in dollars, the value of an activity is measured in dollars. A hobby is less valuable than a job. What George's caretakers hope to do is to give his activity more meaning by attaching a dollar amount to it. It makes no difference to George whether he makes paper angels or wooden boxes—but for most of us, it is the difference between a hobby and a job. If we find meaning only in activities that pay us, then there is a very big draw to do more work. More work equals more value, and more value equals more meaning. Want to have a meaningful life? Work more.

Perhaps the blame for George's situation goes all the way back to his family. Why was he in a home anyway? Shouldn't his parents have been looking after him? Anyone who thinks about it for even a moment knows that this is a complex emotional and ethical situation. We don't hope to do justice to the decisions that face a family like George's except to note two things. First, the same two factors we already talked about—time is money, and work is valuable—are present for every family. Parents must find worthwhile and meaningful activities for their children. If they don't, the kids will fall behind and not be able to keep up or do anything with their lives. All the while, parents must also keep up themselves, finding meaningful and lucrative employment. It doesn't matter what economic class the family belongs to; they need to be busy doing important stuff. This imposed busyness makes for a schedule that feels out of control, going faster and faster while it gets more and more complicated.

George arrives into a family that is already getting pushed to go fast. But he is slow. At some point the simple truth that the whole can only go as fast as the slowest part becomes clear. With any other kid, we would speed them up so that they can keep up. But George can't go faster. Those families face a hard choice. Either slow down to George's speed or find another way that George can live a good life. We recoil against this. In any other situation, we might applaud it when the needs of one don't outweigh the needs of the many, or when the one makes a sacrifice for the good of the whole. But the moral dilemma feels harder in George's case because George doesn't know that he is the one. He doesn't know that he slows down his family, threatens them with his slowness.

The second thing to note is that there are those who do know they are too slow. In fact, many people are too slow for our secular age. We find them at either end of the age spectrum. Babies and the aged, toddlers and the elderly, all move at a different speed. Some of them, the aged, the elderly, and the sick, can remember that they once went fast. They feel like they are a burden. Whether the challenges are physical or mental or a combination thereof, they can't keep up. We find them among the unemployed. These people aren't making money, aren't part of the speed of the world, so they often feel worth less than others. The forced slowdown has caused them to feel worth less than they used to. We notice this among the recently retired. Anyone who has attended the appreciation party and then spoken to that retiree a year later will quickly realize just what slowing down feels like. It's hard. We don't know who we are when we can't keep up.

The story of George reveals truths about our society. It moves fast, faster than many of us can keep up with. Time is money, and money is value. Capitalism assumes that we want more value, thus we need more money—but the choke comes when we realize we cannot make more time. We fill our lives with activities that are supposed to give us value, but there is no end to that quest. Who can have enough meaning? So we go faster and faster and faster. Even the most elite athlete can't run forever. They need to cross a finish line and rest. But society tells us the only finish line is death, so we run and run and run, exhausting ourselves and those around us in the process.

## The Church and the Acceleration of Society

This same acceleration pushes the church as well. Almost every congregation worships once a week, guaranteeing that there are fifty-two events on the calendar. Add in special services at Christmas and Easter plus occasional funerals, and let's say there are a minimum of sixty events per year. But, as youth ministry folks have been saying for years, this time at church pales in comparison to the amount of time the average congregant spends at school or at work or on screens or doing pretty much any of the other meaningful activities they can do. Sixty hours of formation at church per year is nothing compared to the seven hours a day the average American spends looking at a screen. Churches adopt a two-pronged attack to this situation. First, they schedule even more. Weekly age-based programming, outreach, education, alternative forms of worship, retreats, mission trips . . . the list goes on and on. The more you offer the better, because then people can fill their lives with God. Second, they try to smuggle God into all the other activities we do to find meaning. Home, work, and school become even more important. Not only do we find meaning there, but now we must find God there. Neither of these strategies is bad, but both run into a problem: acceleration. We must maximize our time and move fast, and so to fulfill our need for meaning we race from activity to activity. The church has many competitors, and it struggles to elbow out other ways of making meaning.

We came across a good example of this while writing this book. As part of a Lilly Endowment grant called Congregations in a Secular Age, a research team based at Luther Seminary in Minnesota partnered with some congregations and campus ministries to conduct a few experiments. We wanted to see whether there were practices that could not only help people encounter God through encountering another person but also give them language to talk about that experience. A leader from each congregation and ministry came to St. Paul and did a three-day intensive program that involved taking professional-quality portraits and crafting poems about someone else at the meeting. From there, each leader would have their congregation or ministry do something similar, with our team supporting them throughout. Our hunch was that the interventions we planned would help them in a secular age. And the experiment worked! All reported positively on the experience, and while they had reservations about taking three days out of their busy schedules, they were satisfied afterward that it was time well spent.

The next step, running a similar event in their congregation or ministry in cooperation with our team, posed a challenge. A few did it with no problem, but most struggled. They were tired. Trying to keep things going during COVID had sucked out any extra energy they might have had. They couldn't find time on the schedule. Life in ministry is always busy, and there never seemed to be a good time. They couldn't convince their people of the value. All the leaders had been on this retreat beforehand, and all had found it valuable, but that was hard to communicate to others. One of the lessons from this experience was how much busyness dominates us. Acceleration causes fatigue, filling our lives till there is no room left, even if the thing we want to add could be valuable.

We don't blame church leaders for this. They are moving fast, not so that they can get ahead but simply so that they don't fall behind. COVID revealed this, at least in our part of the world. During the pandemic, churches attempted to keep up by moving all the programs and activities online. Clergy and lay leaders alike learned on the fly. Can't worship in person? Get it online! Can't visit the shut-ins or the grieving? Get it online! Can't have fellowship or education events? Get it online! It's all just so exhausting.

### Resonance, Not Slowness

There is always a temptation to romanticize a person like George. If the problem is acceleration, isn't the solution found in the slowness of George? Not exactly. Acceleration, the busyness we feel, is a symptom of our frustrated search for meaning. Treating symptoms only gets us so far. Going slow is likely going to be part of any solution, but it isn't sufficient in itself to solve the problem.

What the story of George points to is the same thing that the early church in Acts 1 shows: waiting. Waiting looks forward to something that is coming. It focuses on the coming of someone who arrives in surprising ways. To really wait means to change our stance. You can't wait when you are busy, caught up in your own project. Who has time to pay attention to someone when there are so many things to do? Both of us play(ed) hockey. How many times have we heard "Keep your stick on the ice!" when doing passing drills? Instead of thinking about what you are going to do next (dreams of "He shoots, he scores!" are so tempting), you need to wait for the puck. If you are not waiting in a ready stance, you'll miss it. So too in life: when we are not waiting in a ready stance, we can miss the important things.

One of the wonderful things about a guy like George is that he was always ready to laugh. Laughter is a response to someone or something else. George could just as easily laugh at a funny face or fart noise as he could at seeing one of his favorite people. His general stance in life was to wait and be ready to laugh. When he first started to get busy it was acceptable, because he could still be ready. But when it got too busy, he couldn't keep up. George laughed less and less because his busyness took all his attention. Even sadder, busyness took his attention but didn't give him anything in return. All he got was more busyness. His Down syndrome placed limits on how fast he could go. In honesty, though, busy individuals and churches also face limits as to how much they can speed up. Just as busyness meant that George couldn't wait anymore, so too we as individuals and churches aren't really in a place where we can wait for God.

The biggest indicator that busyness was stopping George from being ready was that he laughed a lot less. Those encounters with others that gave him delight became few and far between. With less laughing, George got grumpy and moved even slower than he otherwise might have, increasing the pressure put on him to speed up, making him even more busy, leading to less laughter . . . well, you see that it is a vicious circle. Take away the laughter and life becomes much worse, even as you do activities that supposedly bring meaning to your life.

### Sarah: Moving from Ha! to Joy

In the life of the church, laughter is often a sign of God showing up in surprising ways. Perhaps the most famous laugh is Sarah's when God announces that she will have a child in old age. The scene reads like a dark comedy. Sarah and Abraham have not had a biological child despite trying. For whatever reason, Sarah can't get pregnant. Hanging over them are pressures we might identify with, such as family and cultural expectations. Sarah's biological clock is ticking with increasing urgency as attempt after attempt fails. As if that weren't enough, they also face the expectation of a promise that, through their child, God will have a relationship with humans. With that kind of pressure, is it any wonder they struggle to conceive?

Sarah and Abraham find an innovative solution. Abraham will sleep with Hagar, Sarah's handmaid, and that child will count as Sarah's. This is culturally acceptable, and it solves the problem of whatever is going on with their bodies, relieving that pressure. It has the added benefit of bringing a child into the world so that the promises of God will finally happen. One innovative solution solves three problems. What could go wrong?

A lot. And not just of the kind we see in *The Handmaid's Tale*. A son, Ishmael, comes from this union, but from the start Sarah struggles to accept him. Even worse, it becomes clear that this is not the child whom God intended to use to fulfill the covenant. They went to great lengths to find a solution, but in the end everyone got hurt and no one got the benefits from God's promises.

Sarah and Abraham are not bad people. In fact, the opposite. They want to do something for God. The promise of new life is so important that they will do anything to get it. But it is in the doing, not waiting as God told them to, that things get messed up. What they really need to do is wait, but that seems too crazy. Sarah laughs after God says, "I will surely return to you in due season, and your wife Sarah shall have a son" (Gen. 18:10). "Ha!" she says. "I'm going to be pregnant? Really? Haven't we waited long enough? We are too old! Ha!"

At first the laughter comes from a place of surprise, and perhaps not in a good way. It could be that Sarah is saying, "Now? Now you show up? After we've done all these things? Ha! Kind of late, aren't you?" God overhears her laughter. Sarah denies doing it, and the text says she is afraid. In the moment between her reaction of "Ha!" and her subsequent fear of realizing God has overheard it, is it possible that Sarah moves to a deeper place? Is her fear less about what God will do to her because she laughed—condemning her, her actions, her doubt, her surprise—and more about realizing that God can bring life from death, that flourishing can spring from barrenness, that her hopes for herself and all that she loves might actually come true? God does not condemn her laughter; God wants her to own it as the sign of joy in hope.

When Isaac, whose name means "he laughs," arrives in Genesis 21, Sarah says, "God has brought laughter for me; everyone who hears will laugh with me" (v. 6). They won't laugh at her. Nor will her laughter have a cynical tone. It won't be a harsh "Ha!" It will be laughter at the action of God. Who would have thought that Sarah, after years of trying and at one hundred years old, could have a child? Under her own power it was impossible. But God did the impossible. Now we can laugh with joy with Sarah.

If only it were so easy. In a few short paragraphs we move from the failure of innovative change to God acting in surprising ways. Meeting done! The truth is, Sarah was not ready for God, not like George, who was all primed and ready to laugh. She had tried everything in her power to make things work out. When she hears that all of those efforts did not produce what she wanted, her frustration comes out as a "Ha!" She has misdiagnosed the problem as barrenness, and so her solution doesn't solve the real problem. Her imagination can't see what God is doing because what God is doing is so far out there. We tell the story of Sarah less as an exemplar of what to do than an example of how God works. We can take comfort in how God works even as we get frustrated with how long it takes for God to act.

We also can't gloss over the very real suffering that happens because of Abraham and Sarah. Immediately after Sarah's laughter of joy, Hagar and Ishmael are banished. They almost die, crying out to God for rescue. The "solution" to the "problem" is never theoretical. People are never problems or solutions, but in our drive to do something, to make meaning, to get more, we often make them into objects. Even though there is joy at the birth of Isaac, the pain of Ishmael continues. The degree to which George suffers differs from how Hagar and Ishmael suffer, but he still suffers because he becomes a problem to be solved. Likewise for all those who are too slow to be part of the solution. There are good reasons for Abraham and Sarah, and for George's caretakers and family, to do what they do. Those reasons make sense within the secular age, but less so within God's encounter with the world.

Becoming ready for that encounter does involve becoming less busy and focusing on experiences of resonance. But that is not an easy prescription to understand in day-to-day terms. Any easy-to-follow solution about how to encounter God reduces God's presence to a problem. That isn't how the story of Sarah works. In fact, there is quite a bit of confusion even in the encounter in Genesis 21. For instance, it is clear that Abraham hosts someone, but it is not at all clear *whom* he hosts. At one point it is said to be the Lord; at another it is three strangers. Sometimes the subject is the plural "they," and other times the singular "he." Is it God whom Abraham and Sarah encounter? Or is it angels or messengers? Biblical scholars and theologians have argued about this for over two thousand years.

We don't want to attempt to solve this problem here because the confusion rings true to encounters with God that we know about. Whether we cannot see God because the secular age has malformed our imaginations or because it has made us so busy that we cannot see God, when we try to talk about the experience of seeing God, language fails. If we were to ask George to describe his laughter, he couldn't do it. He just knows what he knows, and he laughs when he encounters those he loves. Busyness impedes his laughter, so he knows it is bad but can't explain why. Resonance is slippery like that. We are so used to *doing* that *having* an encounter with God surprises us. We might start with a "Ha!" as Sarah does, but it is possible to move to joy.

# 3

# Stop All the Having and Just Be

## The Moment You're In and the People You're With

In 2019, Aziz Ansari returned to stand-up comedy.[1] It had been a hard year. Ansari had been on the top, part of the popular, award-winning show *Parks and Recreation*, which led to his critically acclaimed series *Master of None*. This was master-piece comedy, the top of the top. And then he was on the bottom, canceled. Bad is bad, and though his behavior wasn't like fellow comedian Louis C.K.'s, and certainly not crimi-nal like other Hollywood figures, it was not good. After he got canceled, he didn't know whether he would ever perform again.

But he did. Ansari returned with his Netflix comedy special *Aziz Ansari: Right Now*. It, too, is a masterpiece. Ansari is still funny, but also different. Gone is the over-the-top hyperactivity.

In its place we meet a more reflective person. The whole set
shows his personal transformation. It builds until we see it
clearly in the final six minutes.

After receiving a roar of laugher, Ansari says, "I want to
thank you all for coming tonight." Pausing for the applause to
die down, he continues, "I really mean that. I really am very
grateful you came. 'Cause, I've done a lot of shows in my career.
At the end of the show, I always go 'G-O-O-D NIGHT and
THANK YOU VERY MUCH.' But the truth is, I never really
meant it." The crowd laughs at this honesty. Ansari continues,
"I was just saying that because that's what you say at the end
of a show. But I really didn't think about what it means that all
you guys came out. But now I think about it in a different way.
Think about it. All you guys drove down here, waited in line.
You did all of this stuff just to hear me talk into a microphone.
And it means the world to me. Because I saw the world where
I never get to do this again."

Ansari is now whispering, and the crowd is hanging on his
every word. "It almost felt like I died. And in a way, I did. The
old Aziz is dead. And I'm glad. Because that guy was always
looking forward to whatever was next. Am I going to do another tour? Am I going to do another season? But I don't think
that way anymore. Because I realized it's ephemeral. All that
stuff can just go away." He snaps his fingers.

Pausing, looking out at the crowd, he says, "All we really
have is the moment we're in and the people we're with. Now, I
talked about my grandma earlier." He told them she had died
in hospice. Taking a breath, he continues, "It's sad. But what
I didn't tell you is that the whole time I was with her, she was
smiling, she was laughing, she was there with me. She was
present in a way no other people I've been around recently have
been. And I've tried to take that with me. Now granted, she

doesn't have much of a choice in the matter. But I do. That's how I choose to live. The moment I'm in with the people I'm with. Right now, this is our moment. So let's take it in."

The theater goes quiet. Everyone sits in silence. A pregnant silence, filled with attention you can feel through the screen. Not something that happens often at church, let alone a stand-up comedy show. After sitting in the quiet, Ansari breaks it and concludes, "And with that, I'll say good night and say thank you very, very much." He smiles and walks offstage.

There it is. That's it. That's the whole thing.

That's what we think your church should do. Or, better, what we think your church should be about.

Okay, we're finished. If that clicks for you, everything falling into place, you can stop reading now. We hope you enjoyed the book. Like Ansari, we're very thankful you've taken the time to read it. Thank you. And good night!

THE END      (roll the credits)

Now that the self-defined geniuses are gone, let's unpack this clip and what it means for the shape of the waiting church.

The whole clip is a parable of what it's like to live in the secular age. The whole situation arose when Ansari coerced a date into sex. Yes, she consented, and so the accusation isn't that he raped her. Still, she left in tears, regretting the experience immediately. Her claim, one that Ansari accepts now, was that she didn't want it, but Ansari wore her down. This is an example of objectification: Ansari treated her as an object rather than a person. Her reluctance made the situation clear. He wanted more pleasure and pursued it. But even if she had fully consented, without regrets, the situation might still have been bad. Two people using each other is also not great.

As Ansari indicates, this event fit the larger pattern of his life. He was always pursuing more. More shows, more roles, more money, more fame, and more pleasure. Each of these pursuits had no end, and they never brought him satisfaction. It was never enough. He would get something and, even in that instant, his mind was on to the next thing. He got called out for seeking more pleasure because it involved objectifying another person, and we still collectively consider that to be wrong. Capitalist societies such as ours rarely call out greed, because the victims stay faceless. Money is an abstraction, an object; a woman on a date shouldn't be, though she was in this case. The logic that drove Ansari to pursue more money was at work the night he pursued more pleasure with his reluctant date.

At one level, we're all like Ansari. Not that we all objectify each other, although that is likely more common than we would like to admit. In chapters 1 and 2, we saw that our lives are always speeding up. We feel the demands to have more and to go faster. As churches, we want more resources and as people, we want the good life, which means more activities that we believe will bring meaning. We turn to effective innovation to help speed ourselves up. Except, like Ansari, it is never enough. We seem to run faster to stay in the same place. Like Ansari before his transformation, we're always looking forward, paying attention to what's next, but not what's in front of us. What coming crisis do we need to maneuver around next? And then next? And then next . . .?

When our crisis is decline—the decline of our churches or falling behind in our life—we feel compelled to do more. This compulsion is real. If we don't do more, our church closes or our life has no meaning. As long as the crisis is decline, we always and forever need to go faster, to do more and more. Is it any wonder we are anxious, stressed, and depressed? Hanging over our heads is the truth that if we don't get things done, we'll fall further behind, sinking deeper and deeper into our hole of decline. Our attention, our deepest concern, must be directed toward a future that our bodies have not yet reached. We spend all of our time throwing ourselves into a hurried future. What an odd way to live. But we barely recognize how weird it is because we're too busy!

All of which supports Ansari's point. Before his transformation, before his little death (we'll return to that soon), his body would be onstage, but his attention would be out ahead of it. His mind would be in some future he needed to race to get to. He couldn't enjoy the moment; he never truly meant his "thank yous." It was hard to have any joy at all. And it was almost impossible to move to gratitude. He was too rushed. As with our churches, Ansari couldn't wait because he needed his rushed actions to win him resources to avoid decline. He needed to keep his mind on the next thing so that his career wouldn't crash.

When we disconnect from what's right in front of us, we end up alienated from ourselves, from the life we're living right now. Disconnecting from the person in front of us harms them because we treat them like an object, and it hurts us too. The secular rush can lead us to stop feeling alive, because we can no longer just *be*. We can no longer just remember and embrace that we're alive, receiving life as a gift. We can't stop and be. We need to move faster and faster to *have* what's out ahead of us. We tell ourselves we don't have a choice. We have to keep our mind on what's next or we'll miss it! Miss what? We're not actually totally sure. We don't even have time to ask such questions. We just know we'll fall behind, and falling behind is a threat.

## Accelerated Action

Ansari thought that the best actors were the busiest actors. Success and busyness went hand in glove. And we bet many of you think this too. The busiest church is the best in town. Whoever has the most programs wins, we assume. Our boards, councils, and sessions figure that the busiest pastor is the best pastor. Many pastors we know assume this too. The pastor rushes, accelerates, trying to get the congregation beyond crisis, pushing others toward an undefined but surely better future. It's so easy to assume that this is best. But it isn't. Acceleration is a disease that promises victory over the crisis of decline but ends in spiritual disaster.

The "good" future is a mirage. Once you get there, there is always another future to chase. You never get to rest. There is never enough, only more. You'll have to keep running until you're totally out of energy and burned-out. How many church boards, councils, and sessions have burned out pastors and church staffs? How many have expectations for the pastor and staff that force them to spend all their energy, dooming them to burnout?

Burnout here is a kind of deadness to the world. There are scholars who believe that the origins of depression in our society come from the fatigue of needing to always be creating, curating, and remaking who we are (see Alain Ehrenberg's *The Weariness of the Self* and Byung-Chul Han's *The Burnout Society*). By "depression" we don't mean strictly clinical depression but rather a deep fatigue, a sense that you just don't have the energy. What we mean is that depression is the body's response to always and forever needing to rush for a future and then the next. Depression sets in when we have no more energy to continue, and yet we still hold the assumption that

42

being busy and having limitless energy is good. Depression (as a social reality) arrives when burnout meets the feeling of moral failure. Both individual people and congregations can become depressed when they're overcome by the need to do more and more but find that they've fallen behind, tapped out of energy to overcome the crisis of decline.

If we closely examine claims about the Sabbath, we can see that such thinking infiltrates our understanding of even that day of rest. Yes, true Sabbath is a good thing, but too often what we think of as Sabbath only plays into this same trap. If we rest so that we can regain our energy, we only drive ourselves deeper into burnout. Rest, true rest, is not simply a chance to recharge our batteries. If you take a Sabbath so that you can work harder the other six days, then the reason you are resting is so that you can do more in the aggregate. Doing more is always the way of acceleration, and it will always end in depression and burnout. If you give your pastor a sabbatical so that they can come back with renewed energy, you are resting within the parameters of effective innovation. The church makes a deal with the pastor—if we give you this time, you will give us more focused energy when you return. At the heart of this warped idea of Sabbath is trying to get more.

## Step 1 in Being, Not Having: Humble Death

Ansari's final six minutes of his show are so powerful because he's left behind this rushing for more and for the next thing. He's escaped by *being*, a much different action from *having*. Getting canceled was more than a wake-up call. It killed his career—and for someone who was always trying to have more, it thereby killed him. He didn't know it, but Ansari began a different relationship with the world that day. He started to *be*, to wait attentively and sense what was going on around him. He focused on the people right in front of him. Ansari discovered what Christians knew before we got too busy to remember: the only way to escape the treadmill of speeding up is to die.

Whoa! That feels intense. It is, but it's not unusual. You're thinking about death all the time, even when you're trying not to think about it. Thinking about death (or trying to avoid it) makes it easy to obsess about the crisis of decline. We think we must rush to get more, because otherwise we won't have the resources for the future. Without these resources, we'll die. Many of you joined the board, council, or session to keep your congregation, or even your denomination, from dying.

We're always thinking about dying, but we don't like to admit it because we hate the thought of dying. Dying is dangerous. It's bad. It goes against what we think God wants. Doesn't God want us to have life and life abundant? Still, when busyness takes over our lives and we feel like we can never stop, it's common to wonder whether the only thing that will stop the treadmill is dying. Burned-out leaders, especially pastors, have wished they could die. Not necessarily suicide, although that is a tragic possibility, but something that simply stops the acceleration. Often they sense that if they ever stop, they'll let down their congregants and they'll disappoint God. They'll betray the faith they have given their life to.

That's heavy, even dangerous, but not uncommon. The COVID pandemic brought us the Great Resignation, which, even if overhyped, at least shows that when faced with a clear existential threat—an uncontrollable disease could kill me— one of our first responses is to quit it all. Thinking about dying (or avoiding thinking about it by getting lost in doomscrolling or drinking or some other way of killing our attention) shows there is something wrong with the way we live our lives. If the only way to stop the acceleration is to die, there is something deeply wrong.

But it's true. Only dying can stop acceleration. There is no other way. Only in dying can the church find its way beyond the crisis of decline, which is a fake crisis, and into the crisis of God's action in the world.

How? There are different kinds of dying. We like to live inside the illusion that we'll never die, so we don't think about the quality of that death. Keep shoving it down, keep denying death, keep moving into the future, keep getting more resources in a hopeless effort to stay alive. But everything made, whether a person, a building, or an institution, dies. This is part of being a creature and not the creator. Creatures, things that are made, die. But there is a good way and a bad way to die. The question is, What kind of death do you want?

We get it, this is heavy. It's intense, particularly for a stand-up comedy set. When Ansari says, "I saw the world where I never get to do this again," he saw a world where he lost all connection to a group of people. For Ansari, this lack of connection felt like a death. He says, "It almost felt like I died. And in a way, I did." But this kind of dying created something new. His death experience led to an honest vulnerability. Or we could say it drew him into humility. Rather than dying in denial, he died in humility. The good death is the one that brings us into humility.

Humility is powerful, but its power is hidden. Humility doesn't seem formidable; it seems like surrender, like giving up. But therein lies its power. Paul tells the Philippian church that humility is foundational to the spiritual life. If the church is a waiting church, following Jesus's command to wait for God's action (Acts 1) starts in humility (Phil. 1). Humility is central to the ethos, or spirit or feel, of a waiting church. Humility is foundational because, Paul tells the Philippians, it is how Jesus lives in the world. Jesus doesn't count equality with God as something to boast about, never as a license for gain. Jesus isn't striving in the world but is simply being in the world, waiting. Jesus humbles himself, emptying himself of all temptation to accelerate and dying to overcome all dying. Paul believes humility is so powerful because it shapes our lives into the form of Jesus's life.

For some, humility might seem easy. There are those who recognize the striving and acceleration of the world but who do not feel like they are personally striving or accelerating. This kind of passive humility can come from outside a person. For instance, for years women have been expected to be passive rather than active. This has forced them into a position that looks like humility. Other times, this kind of passive humility can come from inside a person. There are those who sit happily on the sidelines, letting others take charge, because they themselves no longer have the energy to continually strive.

In both cases, whether passive humility forced from the outside or languishing on the inside, it is false humility. The falseness hinges on what exactly the person is surrendering to. A person forced into "humility" must surrender to the will of the oppressor. But no one can force humility—and in the trying, only humiliation results. Expecting a woman to be passive and then enforcing that takes away her ability to choose to surrender to God. It is sinful, and we must work with God against this kind of oppressive power. We also need to guard against fatalism. Waiting in humility is not tantamount to giving up. It is an act of surrender to God. So if we throw up our hands in despair ("What can I do about it?") or frustration ("I've tried for so long, but nothing works") or resignation ("I can't do it, so I'm done"), we are not actually surrendering to God. We are surrendering to despair, frustration, or resignation.

Humility is not something on our to-do list, as if it were a difficult workout at the spiritual gym. Rather, it is a surrender, stopping and confessing that having more cannot save us or our church. In humility, you confess you need something outside your own energy, outside your own creativity, to save you. You die to yourself by confessing you're in need of a saving you can't accomplish from your own striving for more.

### Step 2 in Being, Not Having: Confession

This kind of dying creates new possibilities because it leads to confession. Ansari confesses that by overlooking both his audience and his art form, he has violated both. Up to this point, it was all about him. He served himself, used people for his own gain. He made success and its financial rewards more important than the connections, than *being with*. He made what's next more important than the moment of being with his audience. It all became about what's next, not what is.

Celebrity apologies are a staple of news and social media. It's a big deal how public figures respond to failure and blowback. There seem to be two possible responses. One is to admit full-throated that you were totally and completely wrong. You grovel a little (but not too much lest you seem fake), making sure that everyone knows you've learned from your mistake. Coming to mind for you might be the seemingly daily example of someone else going down this way by apologizing for an unwise statement.

The second way to respond to blowback is to never, ever say you're wrong. You stare down the accusation and never blink. If you never admit you're wrong, never apologize, then the blowback can't land. This is an unapology apology. At the proverbial water cooler or on the twenty-four-hour news, we

47

talk about why this person can't just admit they're wrong. A few politicians of note are very good at this. They seem to turn the blowback around, spinning it back onto those who started it.

Ansari does neither of these. He doesn't apologize; he confesses. He's not looking to manage the blowback but to live differently. Unlike an apology, a confession moves to restoration. Where an apology tries to avoid the vulnerability of restoration, a confession, at least in the Christian faith, seeks connection. Confession is a move to repair a broken relationship. In a legal context, justice needs a confession. The confession—letting go, stopping, admitting, and waiting—is the way to be placed back in a connection with others whom you've hurt or overlooked.

Jesus calls the church in Acts 1 to wait. But wait for what? To wait for the deep connection with God. The connection is so deep it is spirit to Spirit. At its core, the church is a confessing community because it is a waiting community. A confession is much deeper than an apology.

One thing that makes Ansari's final six minutes so powerful is that they start in confession. And so too should your board, council, or session. The first thing to do is to confess together that you are more captivated by the crisis of decline than by the crisis of God's action. That what you want is not a waiting church but an accelerating church. And that this wanting has far more to do with your own anxiety than with your trust in God. We need to confess that our attention has been on accelerating to ward off decline or to achieve gain rather than on attending to the connections right before us. We need to confess that we've led the church by leaving the present for what's next instead of breathing in the joy of the connections of the community and beauty of the gospel. We've wanted to speed up rather than wait inside the gift of these beautiful connections.

## Step 3 in Being, Not Having: Gratitude

When we confess and someone else receives it, even when it is a small connection, the response of the confessor is gratitude. It's saying, "Thank you!" The confession makes a connection. The confessor is seen and heard in their humility. That's powerful! Humility binds this power, stopping it from being a power play. Confession does not take away the wrongs, but it is necessary for any real justice, reconciliation, and restoration. The only possible response from the confessor is gratitude for being heard and seen, for connecting with another person.

We know Ansari is not apologizing but confessing because the whole six minutes revolve around gratitude. He wants to say a true "thank you" for the connections, for being in this present moment, at this time, with these people, the very people he's overlooked. He wants to thank them for the privilege it is to be connected to his art and share it with others. Ansari confesses he hasn't always served that connection. He's been selfish. But in receiving their forgiveness, through their participation, his response is to say thank you. Because of this confession there is the possibility of repair, of a new connection that can give life to all of them.

We should not let Ansari off the hook. His dying, humility, and confession have limits. The incident that started all of this involved a woman, and truth be told, we don't know whether Ansari confessed to her. While the audience recognizes his confession, even giving him some form of absolution by coming and watching him, we should not expect that others whom he has sinned against will do the same. The gratitude Ansari feels in this moment does not mean that he can stop dying, humbling himself, and confessing. Quite the opposite. Now that he has seen his sin of not living in the moment with these people, in alienating himself from his audience and his art, he can see that this also happens in other parts of his life. Dying in humility, confessing, is not a one-time event but continual.

Gratitude in confession does not stem from absolution, which depends on someone else and may never come. Ansari's confession might lead to absolution, but even if it doesn't, he can still offer it in gratitude. Gratitude comes from being seen and heard in the moment of humble death, not from what we get out of it. Gratitude is the gift of being able to confess, not what the confession wins you. At the root of gratitude is connection, in being with these people in this place, in vulnerability, in need. This runs counter to our culture, which focuses on getting past that moment of vulnerability to the moment when we can focus on getting more. We have all seen someone "confessing" because they want to work their way back from getting canceled. When someone apologizes basically for getting caught, it tells us that they don't want confession, they want absolution. Often, we think that the source of gratitude is those things in our life worthy of the hashtag #blessed. Gratitude actually comes from being in this vulnerable moment with these people with our own sin exposed. How good is it for the people of God to dwell together? Very good, because in moving from having to being, to dying, humbling ourselves, and confessing, we dwell not only with each other. We dwell with God.

## Being, Not Having, the Waiting Church

A waiting church is waiting for God, waiting for the Spirit to move, and waiting to connect with God. Our crisis becomes the crisis of God's action. As we wait for God's action, we open ourselves to God's arriving by ministering to one another. In humility, we attend to our connections. We do this by concerning ourselves with the present, which is the only place where we live out our connections. We live with others in the present, not the future. Tending to connections and relationships is how we live faithfully in the present, in the right now.

We attend to these connections in humility. In humility, we enter death by hearing confessions, inviting one another to speak of our death experiences. We confess the ways that others, our circumstances, or our own choices have thrust us into loss. We hear each other share these stories and we receive them. These confessions of loss and longing connect us. We're released from acceleration, which only wants us to spend energy for future resources, when we confess our loss and need in the now. Here we're together. Here we're alive. And we respond with gratitude. The confession that is made, heard, and shared connects us deeply. We live in the now by saying "thank you."

Church boards, councils, and sessions should lead their congregations by confession and gratitude. Your job, as you wait for God's arrival, is to tend to the connections of the community. Focus on the relationships. Find waiting wrapped in those relationships. You do this *not* by thinking you can replace God, not by believing it's up to you to secure the church's future. No. You do this by teaching others and creating space for confession and gratitude. The waiting church is a church led in humility into confession and thankfulness. The waiting church lives in the now by gratitude. This is how we're alive and attentive to the arrival of God.

Even if this doesn't sound too abstract to you, it might sound too hard. "Successful" churches and denominations in North America have recently gone under the microscope. What we heard in *The Rise and Fall of Mars Hill* podcast or read about in the Guidepost Solutions report outlining sexual abuse allegations and responses within the Southern Baptist Convention

(SBC) is pretty damning.[2] While the details are important, especially recognizing that these victims told the truth but the church ignored them, both stories share some commonalities. Mars Hill and the SBC are shining examples of accelerated growth, of having but not being. Both made their name by being the fastest-growing church or denomination, for having the most resources, most people, and most influence.

Mars Hill was a megachurch that grew at a phenomenal rate in what is supposed to be one of the most secular cities in the US: Seattle. It amassed more resources, more people, more influence, all so that secular people might know Jesus Christ. In reality, though, Mars Hill was little different from other successful companies in Seattle. The strategy driving Mars Hill would not have been out of place at Microsoft or Boeing or Amazon. The drive to accelerate meant that relationships served the larger goal of more. When those relationships stopped producing the growth the church required, the people got, in senior pastor Mark Driscoll's words, "run over by the bus."

Upon firing two church elders, Driscoll told a conference, "There is a pile of dead bodies behind the Mars Hill bus [he chuckles], and by God's grace, it'll be a mountain by the time we're done. You either get on the bus or you get run over by the bus. Those are the options. But the bus ain't going to stop!" Accelerate at all costs! Past the bombastic nature of this statement, which is pretty scary coming from a church leader, lies an even darker truth. When the image of the church is a speeding bus that will not stop even for its own leaders, we know that the logic of acceleration has captured our imagination. For Driscoll, the ends justified the means, and the ends in this case were more people, more resources, and more influence. We get rid of deadweight to find more leaders, we spend money to make more money, we build a bigger platform to gain influence.

It's the same logic in the business world. Is it any wonder that Mars Hill was wildly "successful" in Seattle when it so closely mimicked "successful" secular businesses?

Likewise, the SBC has long prided itself on being the largest, fastest-growing Protestant denomination in the United States. What the Guidepost Solutions report shows is that all levels of SBC leadership ignored, diminished, and suppressed a staggering number of credible allegations of sexual abuse. Again, the ends justified the means. Leaders accused of sexual abuse were doing good things in the eyes of other leaders and therefore needed protection. How would the church grow if we held these leaders accountable? Further, how would it look if the truth became public? Wouldn't that threaten the growth of the church? Time after time after time, leaders ignored victims of sexual abuse and further traumatized them to protect the church's need for more people, more resources, and more influence.

Mars Hill and the SBC are not unique, but they are obvious examples of what happens when the church's imagination gets captured by the secular logic of acceleration. To stay alive, to thrive, they need more people. The idea of dying is completely foreign to this way of thinking, even if it is at the core of the gospel. To gain more influence, they must look successful. Never mind that their understanding of success never leads to humility but pride. So that donors continue to give the resources required, the church must admit no sin or weakness. This flies in the face of the basic call to repent, to confess, to be present in this moment and with these people. Not every church that buys into the logic of acceleration will have such a fall from grace as Mars Hill or the SBC. But when the ends justify the means, every church that buys into this logic of acceleration cannot encounter a God who comes to us in Jesus Christ by the power of the Holy Spirit.

For some, these might be harsh words. Even if you agree with our analysis, leading people into death, humility, and confession seems impossible, because those actions run counter to the secular imagination that fuels so much of what we consider successful. Perhaps there is another way into the waiting church. Ansari's confession and gratitude do stem from his experience of death, but there are really two deaths at work in his life. The first was the death of his career, his alienation from the audience and his art. The other was the death of his grandmother. If the first one resulted from his own sin, the second was an invitation from someone he loved. Perhaps the stories of Mars Hill and the SBC fit into the first category. Such a death might lead to confession and gratitude, but as a leader, it would be much easier if there were another way than implosion. Maybe a dying grandmother offers a different path.

## An Invitation to the Waiting Church

Ansari's confession and his move into gratitude came as a result of his own shortcomings but also from the loss of his grandmother. Watching her as she lived, even as he waited with her for her death, changed him. Her death opened him up to something deeper. In the humble way she faced her death and her joy at just being present with Ansari, his grandmother showed him a way into transformation. Ansari's grandmother gave him a new way of life, one that places no value on acceleration. This way does not avoid decline but faces death head-on. It doesn't look to extend the future but to face the end. It's a way of life that is grounded in the now. In our language, it's a *waiting* way of life: waiting deeply with others.

Meaning fills this kind of waiting. It is not a lonely waiting. It would be a sad, even dehumanizing, waiting if Ansari's grandmother had been left all alone to die, stored away out of sight and out of mind. That waiting is destructive and pained. Alone, we have nothing to wait for, and in that, waiting is unnatural, even demonic. Her waiting is with and for others. She invites Ansari to wait with her, to be with her in this moment, to honor and lean into their connection. This kind of waiting is the antidote to alienation. This kind of waiting is what Jesus calls the church to in Acts 1.

This waiting is all about *this moment with these people*. It might look like this way of life has no direction, but it offers a new direction, a new way of life. As Ansari says, this is his new way of being in the world. His life is now all about *this moment with these people*. He even leads his audience into the practice. Like a pastor, he gently ushers them into silence. (Not something you often see at a comedy show!) He invites his audience to breathe and just be in this moment. To recognize that they are with these people. Like many stand-up comedians, during the show he interacts with the audience, learning some names and making them part of the show. Then, at the end, he calls out the names of some in the audience, directing people to see them in that moment. Names learned in the service of laughs now anchor the audience in a deeper relationship. Ansari calls them to attend to the connections as they wait together in both silence and laughter. They're no longer an audience but a congregation, even a community, in those moments.

This is what a waiting church does. It attends directly and passionately to this moment with these people. It finds life not by giving attention to the future and the resources needed to escape decline but by stewarding those connections. In stewarding the connections, the future will take care of itself. Boards, councils, and sessions lead by inviting the congregation to attend to this moment with these people, trusting that we prepare ourselves for—maybe even experience—the presence of the living God. In this waiting, we don't do nothing, bored and disconnected. We do the most important thing. We give our people a way of life that is all about *this moment with these people.*

The invitation to wait is no less difficult to hear than it is to be confronted by the fact that the secular age has captured our imagination and we need to die. But at least it is calling us to something that everyone can see as meaningful. Even if they cannot articulate all the reasons, our society knows that to be with a dying loved one is important. Our greatest regret is often that we weren't there. This feeling need not turn to regret. It can turn to an action: waiting. Not that either Ansari or his grandmother is a saint. His routine is filled with examples that might make you scratch your head and say, "What do these guys see in Ansari?" Fair enough. Still, it is all the more miraculous because they aren't saints. Their connection is imperfect. Ansari may not always maintain this stance of being rather than having. But now he knows another way. He knows about dying, confessing, being humble, and having gratitude. He has had a taste of connection and something more. And this experience can and has changed his life, even if this change is not yet complete.

### Resonance: Worship and Prayer

The waiting church is one of worship and prayer, because none of us is perfect. In Acts 1:14, we see the disciples "constantly devoting themselves to prayer" as they wait for the Holy Spirit. Worship and prayer are not magic. They do not summon God. God doesn't work for us! Worship and prayer are the silent and spoken union of attending to this moment with these people. Worship and prayer are the ways of life that seek a connection with God in a community. It is here that we wait, week by week.

This is how we wait for the living God. We wait by attending not to our resources or relevance but to this moment with these people—seeking God together.

Another name for this kind of waiting is *resonance*. Resonance is both the action of seeking connections and the result of that seeking. It is a way of being in the world that stays in the present because it doesn't get distracted by the future of more. It seeks not growth but depth, participation, and union. Resonance is action that awaits arrival. Resonance has no illusions about possessing the world—or even God—it acts to receive, to wait for what is uncontrollable. The best parts of life, the actions that change us, are uncontrollable, coming to us as the actions of resonance. We must wait for them. Experiencing a confession of love, reaching for a friend, witnessing a beautiful sunset—they all connect us, but we can never control them. By waiting and receiving, we act. We wait for what is uncontrollable by attending to *this moment with these people*. We trust that inside this moment with these people we'll encounter, at some point, a resonance that will connect us deeply with the world and the God who loves this world.

With other leaders in your church, read the following case study and answer the question that Jake poses at the end, "What should they do?"

## Red Paint

Jake looked at the doors of the church where he served, Grace Presbyterian. As the minister responsible for community engagement, he often came in and out of these doors. Though not always practical because of the many steps, they were important.

They opened onto the main street, acting as a link between the community and the church. He had not expected to see them today. It was a holiday, July 1, so he was off for Canada Day. That was until his wife showed him her Twitter feed with a picture of the church. "Isn't this Grace?" Yes, yes it was. He hoofed it to the big downtown church as fast as he could. When he got there, the large wooden doors were still dripping with red paint that had been splashed on the doors to look like blood.

He had seen that this was not an isolated incident. Other churches in different parts of the country had similar scenes that morning. Anglican, United Church, and Roman Catholic churches. Not a coincidence. All four of these churches had run residential schools. In partnership with the government, the churches had run schools for Indigenous children. The first ones opened in the 1870s, a few years after confederation, and the last one didn't close until the 1990s. Jake knew that the red paint was about those schools.

Like many Americans, Jake was unfamiliar with the residential school system till he worked for a Canadian church. Even then, despite the Truth and Reconciliation Commission, the prime minister apologizing in the House of Commons, and the denomination's own efforts to reconcile with Indigenous people, the residential schools were not a key part of the story told about Canadian history.

For some, that was then and this is now. As long as they weren't racist today, they didn't understand why they needed to get worked up about what their ancestors did. For others, they viewed the residential schools' intentions as good but considered the church and the government's approach to be flawed. The hope was that Indigenous people would assimilate into the main culture, lifting them out of poverty and ensuring they were productive members of society.

Jake knew that both of these responses were flawed. Even though he was not Canadian, he felt a responsibility as a Christian and a minister for what was done in Christ's name in the past. And he knew that good intentions that lead to evil consequences are not really good. Indigenous groups had called on the church to recognize that assimilation was a form of cultural genocide. The point of the schools was to destroy the old ways of speaking and being, replacing them with the white ways of talking and working.

The recent events in Kamloops had brought all of this back into the public eye. Through the dogged efforts of Indigenous leaders who never doubted their elders when they said that children had disappeared from the residential school in Kamloops, over two hundred unmarked graves were found. It was front-page news, and people were angry. Even some in the church. Popular Christian artist Brian Doerksen partnered with Indigenous singer Cheryl Bear to write "215," a searing indictment of the government and the church. Jake had watched the music video online, and he knew a reckoning was coming.

Now here it was. On his doorstep. The red paint was still wet as he stood there, wondering what he should do. He took out his phone and called his elders. This was important enough to call an emergency meeting. But he wondered, what should they say or do?

# 4

# It's Time to Wait, but for What?

## Parking Lots and Road Rage

Our kids, at various stages of development, loved the strangeness of the English language: we drive on parkways and park on driveways. Anyone who has recently driven in an urban area might question the first of those statements. Parkways seem to have so many cars and so many stoplights that they more closely resemble parking lots than freeways. The same is true for roads, alleys, highways, byways, and that shortcut that used to work but doesn't since they installed traffic-calming measures and a stoplight. The car, something that should speed up your life, ends up being a place where we wait.

And that waiting is. so. painful. There are stages to the pain. First, as your car slows to a stop, your brain begins down the path, "Oh, wh . . ." and before you can even get a thought together, an internal alarm goes off. You need to do something, anything, instead of thinking about waiting. Grab your phone. Even though it is illegal and dangerous, you check your email yet again. Some part of you knows that in the five minutes since you started driving there is no chance that you got an email, let alone an email you care about, but you check anyway because if you don't, you might have to consider why you are waiting in the first place.

The second stage moves from distracting your impatience to trying to find the cause of the slowdown. Is there a crash up there? A big transport truck? Congestion? Construction? You check the real-time map on your phone, trying to see whether anyone else has reported the slowdown. You might pull to the side so you can see further down the line of traffic. Are those sirens in the distance? Unbelievable, your mind thinks, 'cause now you feel like you are stuck behind a sixty-two-car pileup and the emergency vehicles are on their way. How long will you have to wait now?

The third stage moves to anger and blame. How did that idiot ahead of you get a license! The half-witted city council keeps approving all of these stupid lights! Can't they do this construction at a more convenient time? I WANT TO GET HOME! Other drivers take the brunt of your anger, but everyone from the street cleaner to the mayor could end up in your sights. We don't use the gun reference lightly. Road rage can turn violent.

Maybe these three stages are not you. Perhaps waiting in the car does not faze you, does not move you to anger. But you also might be strange. We do not like to wait. There are three reasons. First, we have somewhere to go. We have a goal and we can't get there. Like a toddler who can see the cookies and moves quickly to grab more, we don't like to hear the word "no." Second, we cannot control what stops us. On a smaller scale, we have to accept that other drivers make good or bad decisions. On a larger scale, when we get in the car, we take part in a much larger system. Economics (buying a car, gas, etc.) and politics (laws, planning, etc.) shape our driving experience. We feel like we have to own a car to do the things we need and want to do. No one person makes the driving rules, and so we have to give in to the stupid decisions that others make.

The third and final reason why waiting moves to rage, especially in the car, is that we are alone. Even when we're not driving by ourselves, our anger turns us outward, away from whoever is next to us in the moment. The waiting leads to anger, which means that if we do interact with other people in the car, most often a spouse or a kid, it is snippy and short. What a wasted moment! Instead of saying, "Oh, we can't get there any faster, why don't we take this time to have a real conversation," we obsess about what we are missing and the things that cause us to wait. Speeding up blinds us to what is going on right in front of us. Like the old Smashing Pumpkins song says, "Despite all my rage, I am still just a rat in a cage."

### Titling a Sequel

As we said in chapter 2, we think that Luke's sequel, the Acts of the Apostles, is mistitled. Luke's first book—his Gospel—is named after him, as with Matthew, Mark, and John. The author's name is used as the title of the Gospel. But what do you do when there's a part two? How do you title the sequel? *Star Wars* is a great title—*The Empire Strikes Back* an amazing title. It gives you an alluring snapshot of the story you're about to watch.

Despite Hollywood's desire to turn good stories into money-making machines, not all good stories call for a sequel. Unlike

Matthew, Mark, and John, who didn't write a part two, Luke has more to say. He wants to share what happens after the resurrection. And there is an audience. Theophilus, the audience for part one, is ready for the sequel.

As we mentioned earlier, the New Testament authors did not title their own books. That came a few hundred years later. The church fathers, bishops, and monks titled the books, including Luke's. Calling them First Luke and Second Luke was an option. They had made such a decision with plenty of other books in the New Testament. But those "First" and "Second" titles are for epistles, letters. Far from writing letters, Luke writes stories. Actually one big story in two parts. He has a sequel in mind from the very beginning: part one isn't complete without part two.

Our collective movie watching is broad enough that we know there are a few ways to start a sequel. You can start it with a time jump, usually jumping forward in time. Part one has ended, and the sequel begins with something like "Four Years Later." Sometimes there is a jump backward in time, giving a backstory. The hero of part one is a child, or there's a flashback to the city that had been destroyed but at an earlier time was happy. Sometimes there is no time jump at all. Part two starts *exactly* where part one ended. Usually there is even a little overlap between the end of part one and the beginning of part two, to remind us where we left off. That's how Luke starts his sequel.

## Ending Together, Beginning Together

Luke's Gospel ends with two followers on the road to Emmaus (Luke 24:13–35). These two are not main characters, not part of the inner circle. Neither end up as apostles. They don't make it to the sequel. Yet, they followed, putting their hope and love in Jesus. And now Jesus is dead. These two disciples are distraught. Their hope is dashed, hearts filled with sorrow. They need to get away and figure out what's next. They start with a debrief.

Luke tells us that seven miles outside of Jerusalem—seven is a number draped in meaning—a fellow traveler joins them. This mysterious fellow traveler wants to know what they are talking about. Like you telling someone about the horrible traffic, they need to tell the story. They're shocked that this stranger doesn't already know. Has he not checked Twitter? Their conversation goes deep. As they get to their destination, they invite the traveler to join them for a meal, to come and rest. They would wait together for the morning. In the middle of their meal of waiting, this mysterious traveler breaks bread, and it's revealed to them. A veil is lifted; a revelation comes. This is the resurrected Jesus. And then Jesus is gone. In the waiting, he's revealed and then hidden.

That same hour the two hoof it back to Jerusalem. They tell Peter and the others what they've seen. Shortly, they all see Jesus, who greets them with a word, "Peace," and then he is with them. As with the two, they all eat and recline, resting in each other's presence. Jesus promises to send the Spirit from on high before he ascends, leaving the disciples worshiping him in joy.

Part two starts with a shout-out to Theophilus and a line about why Luke feels compelled to write the sequel, but then we are right back where part one ended. There's no gap between the end of part one and the start of part two. Luke tells Theophilus that many followers saw Jesus over those forty postresurrection days (another mysterious, symbolic number— Israel wandering for forty years, Jesus in the desert for forty days). Luke reminds Theophilus what happened right after the road to Emmaus, that Jesus appeared to the disciples in Jerusalem. There Jesus gave them a direct command—which we believe creates the church—as they're just *being* together. They're eating, sharing, and reclining. Jesus tells them, "Do not leave Jerusalem but *wait*"! "Wait for the gift my Father promised, which you have heard me speak about. For John baptized with water, but in a few days you will be baptized with the Holy Spirit" (Acts 1:4–5 NIV).

Wow! Amazing. So amazing it's easy to focus on what happens after the command more than the command itself. It's like giving your seven-year-old the command, "Go to sleep," followed by, "Because after you sleep, you'll awake to a tree surrounded by presents." The command to sleep is completely overshadowed by the promise of the presents. The promise actually makes it very hard to obey the command to sleep. Yet we shouldn't miss that Jesus gives the command to *wait*. Wait for God to act. Not for the apostles to act. The apostles are to wait. God is the actor. The apostles will act, sure, but only out of their waiting. Only after waiting and receiving a gift will they act. Their action is only in response to God's action.

## It Begins in Waiting Together

The church begins with the command to wait. Now we want to add that we wait *together*. For the disciples, waiting becomes a kind of being, filled with eating and storytelling, praying and remembering, all in anticipation and as preparation for God's action. It's no different today. The church—like the one you're helping to lead—often feels like it's in a painful standstill. We assume there is something we're supposed to do, something other than wait for the action of God. Too often we believe there is something else we should be doing than being together, eating, storytelling, praying, and remembering, rehearsing again and again the story of Jesus Christ's life and its meaning. Yet, it's only out of this being together, this waiting, that we encounter the living God. In encountering this living God we are called out into the world to follow this God who loves the world (John 3:16).

Go-getters, even a group of go-getters, have good intentions that lead to bad things. They want to save the church, but in trying to do so, they condemn it to miss God's action. The Spirit does not come to go-getters. Rarely does the Spirit come to the hurried who are seeking more and more. Rather, the Spirit comes to waiters (to people who wait, although, sure, the Spirit can come to people who take your order at a restaurant, but that's not really what we mean). The church doesn't need go-getters, even though we idealize such people in this moment of decline and fear.

Peter has this go-getter tendency in him. As a good leader, a man of action, Peter confidently tells Jesus that he would never ever deny him. Jesus knows better (Luke 22:31–34). By dawn Peter denies him three times (22:54–62). In Jesus's last days, the man of action, the go-getter, cannot follow the action of God. We are to wait for the Holy Spirit. Peter can only be the rock the church is built on because he's been (painfully) taught to wait.

## Anxious Church Admin

Luke tells us one story before the arrival of the Spirit in Acts 2. It's a story of the apostles busily acting instead of waiting. They are commanded to *wait*, and they do. For a while. We're told that after Jesus's ascension they return to their upper room in Jerusalem. They wait. They pray. The church is created by Jesus's command to wait as prayer, and prayer as waiting. The church, at its core, is a people who wait and pray, pray and wait (all through storytelling, which we will come to later).

But then, maybe like you reading this chapter, they get antsy. In Acts 1:12–26 Peter starts getting twitchy. He starts feeling a little like you do in traffic, looking at your phone, checking out what's going on out the window. He wants to get somewhere, to do something, and all this waiting doesn't seem to be going anywhere. To cope with the agitation Peter decides it's time for some *church administration*. You know how that goes! This has been happening for over two thousand years. When the church feels the heavy burden of the command to wait for God to act, inside the uneasy waiting, it becomes easy to distract ourselves with meetings, procedures, polities, and more. We can claim that the church indeed starts in Acts 1 with the command to wait, because it's during this time that the first church administration meeting happens.

Peter tells the group gathered that they need a replacement. With Judas Iscariot dead, they need a new apostle. It's time to do a staff hire. They're commanded to wait, but what better way to wait, Peter assumes, than to get resources and fill the empty staff position? They need a twelfth (another mysterious number). But instead of using LinkedIn, they go Vegas on it and nominate two people and cast lots to determine which one. It lands on Matthias. He's the new apostle!

We never hear about him again. Nada.

They were supposed to wait, not administrate. Like a pregnant woman in her last trimester, when waiting is hardest, we feel compelled to organize. This casting of lots, rolling the dice, is the acts of the apostles, not the act of God. They do not get in trouble with God, but their action doesn't lead anywhere. It was kind of useless, a distraction, unnecessary to the larger goal of the church. It's the act of the apostles that chooses Matthias.

No hate directed toward Matthias, but he's chosen before the Spirit arrives, and he quickly disappears from Luke's sequel of the acts of God.

In Acts 9, with no apostles present, we're told of God's own action of choosing. God elects the twelfth not by rolling dice but through an interrupting encounter with words and visions. On the road to Damascus, a zealot named Saul is knocked to the ground and addressed by Jesus. The rest of Luke's sequel is about this Saul, renamed Paul. The one chosen by the Spirit, not by the disciples' casting of lots, is at the center of Luke's acts of God. The acts of the apostles choose Matthias; the act of God elects Paul. The dice choose Matthias; the living, resurrected Jesus chooses Paul.

## God Chooses Saul

In Acts 9:11 we hear that Saul, after being encountered by Jesus, goes to a different Judas's house on a street called Straight.[1] What is he doing? He's *waiting*. He's blind and shaken from the encounter. All he knows is where to go and what to do: wait. The reader of the story finds out that he waits for the Spirit to call Ananias. Ananias, called a disciple, is told to go to Paul. He does so as a representative of the church. Ananias was waiting in prayer. It does not make much sense to him, but Ananias, in his own waiting, hears God's call and goes and waits and prays with Paul.

Paul was on that road in hurried action. He was rushing to protect his religion, ready to kill people like Ananias. But now he's in Judas's house in forced waiting. Ananias, one of those he was going to kill, is called out of his waiting by God to come and wait with Paul. In this risky waiting, Paul is invited to *be* with and in the church. From within this waiting with Ananias, who shares Paul's confusion and pain, Paul is sent into the world with the story of an encounter with the resurrected Christ.

The title of Luke's sequel is all wrong. It's not the Acts of the Apostles but the Acts of God. The apostles wait; God acts. When they don't wait, it isn't the end of the world, but nothing is really accomplished. The apostles act only because God moves them out of their waiting. Yes, they go and do things, and they lead others in doing things, but they always return to waiting. There is a deep sense that God is at work in the world, doing things we cannot see because we are so busy. Through waiting, the church is sent out into joining the acts of God. Waiting shapes the church to be, solely by the acts of God.

## Waiting Doesn't Suck

But hold on, waiting sucks! Isn't that what the getting-stuck-in-traffic parable above says? True. Waiting sucks so much that we'll even choose church administration instead of waiting.

However, waiting only sucks when you have the wrong story. The disciples are never called to wait storyless. Peter and the disciples are the church *not* through church administration but through the stories of Jesus's own life, death, and resurrection. The church is birthed and called to wait because it is always to be looking for the living Jesus Christ's action in the world. For the church, waiting is the way of attentive looking. The church must wait because its *only* job is to witness to the living Jesus Christ, who is moving in the world. In Acts 1 the church is commanded to wait before it goes into the world so it can have the Spirit to empower it (not for world domination) to see the living and moving Jesus in the world. Rolling dice don't choose Paul; Jesus does, not by chance but in an encounter that blinds Paul, forcing him to wait till he can finally see. When he opens his eyes, he sees what he couldn't before: this crucified, poor Galilean is the salvation of the world. Paul must wait to see that Jesus lives. Paul must wait to get the story right.

Your grandmother or elementary school librarian taught you to never judge a book by its cover. But a title does give you a sense of what to expect. We critique the title of Luke's sequel because it's not accurate to what's really happening in the book. We're not trying to be rock-and-roll, cool iconoclasts—that's not us (particularly *not* Blair). We actually love those old bishops and monks who chose the title. We don't want to throw shade on them (that was Andy trying to be cool). But titles can shape stories. And stories shape us. And how we're shaped by stories has a direct impact on the life of the church.

### The Star of the Story

Let's get back in the car. In traffic. You get angry because you have somewhere to go. There is a story there. You are traveling to your kid's soccer game. Or a meeting. Or the doctor. Wherever it is, you want to get there for some reason, and that reason fits within a larger series of reasons that, all put together, make up the story of your life. You are not unique. All the other people around you have stories that lead them somewhere. Some of their stories are better than yours. They are going to more important places or have more exciting things to do than you. Whatever the case, you both face the same enemy—this stupid, pointless waiting. Actually, every anxious and angry person scattered across traffic has a story about needing to get going. Each person's story places that person—their own plans and worries—as the star of that story. Waiting is the enemy in each story. You are the hero, and waiting is the antihero of this story you're living while in this motionless chunk of metal.

Anxiety and anger have a way of committing us to a story where our own needs and wants take center stage. This is a physiological fact. Anxiety triggers our fight-or-flight reflex, and anger sends us hurtling down the fight path. When we're in fight-or-flight mode, our attention is *only* on our own survival. In the car it's impossible to wait contentedly, let alone see waiting as a gift, because you're anxious. And because you're anxious everything in you wants to run or throw punches. Hello, road rage. Your muttered stories, your snippiness with the kids, is all about you! *You* need to get where *you* are going. Sure, other people around you might have better stories, but you're too anxious to put down your own story and consider that. You're way too anxious to take a supporting role in any story. If the thought enters your mind about what that other guy is going to do, it quickly vanishes so you can assure yourself that your story is the most important because . . . well . . . it's about you. He's a stranger. You, and you alone, are the star of the anxious tale you're living. You're too anxious for it not to be all about you.

Perhaps you don't drive. Or you love to drive because you get to listen to podcasts and audiobooks. Fair enough. What about waiting for someone to email you back? Or, even more urgently, to text you? We remember the days when we had to write something down, find an envelope, stick a stamp on it, go to the mailbox, and then wait. Letters took days, maybe weeks, which meant waiting for days, maybe weeks, for a reply. With email and texting, though, we can have an almost instantaneous response. Because of the possibility of an instant response in an accelerated world, we expect an instant response. The hurried anxiety tumbles out: Why isn't that person texting me back? Are they in trouble? Do they not love me? Am I getting ghosted!? The expectation that they would text us back immediately comes from the acceleration we all feel; the anxiety comes from the fact that we are the stars of our own stories.

As we've mentioned, we both *were* hockey players. Now we're too old. We still watch a lot of hockey, but now our sport is dog walking. We're both pretty into it. If ESPN or TSN televised dog walks, we'd probably watch. Dogs are a different kind of glorious beast. They interact with us in a way that no other animal does. Hence, they can be taken on walks. And *love* it. Most other pets, not so much. It's rare, even weird, to see a cat on a leash, tail wagging happily on a walk, excited to get to the park. This is because all animals (except humans and their dogs) function primarily in fight-or-flight mode. Constantly living in a quick-trigger, fight-or-flight existence, among other reasons, means that animals are not storied creatures like us. Needing to quickly trigger fight or flight, animals particularly don't seem to have the cognitive capacity to enter into our stories. We love dogs so much because they mystically enter our stories. They are the perfect wingmates.

Stories can take on greater importance when we enter into another's story. That story, one in which we are not the star, can shape our own life in a fundamental way. We find deep fulfillment in being a supporting part of another person's story. This happens all the time for parents. At the very least, humans recognize—when not too stressed or annoyed—that other humans live different stories that give them a different perspective on a situation we are all living in. Like the guy in the car next to you. He's experiencing the traffic much differently. He's hoping the cars sit on the parkway for another hour. He wants to get stuck. Tensions between him and his wife are so fraught that the thought of another hour away feels better than making it home to his frigid bedroom. Imagine all the other stories in all the other cars.

The title of Luke's sequel matters because it frames who is the star of the church's story. Whether it's the Acts of the Apostles or the Acts of God offers two very different answers about who is the primary star of this story. The common belief is that the church begins in Acts 2, with Pentecost. We contend that the church begins in Acts 1, with waiting. With its origin in Acts 1, we can see that the church *cannot* be the star of its own story. When we read Acts 1 and 2 together, we see that not only is the church not the star of its own story; it's not even a primary protagonist.

The contrast between Matthias and Paul makes this clear. Church administration chooses Matthias; Jesus Christ chooses Paul. We're sure that Matthias was important and faithful, possessing such qualities the apostles were looking for. Some church administration is necessary and welcome; sometimes it's even the work of the Holy Spirit. But Luke has nothing else to say about Matthias while the whole rest of the sequel is about Paul. Not because Paul is better, more talented, or more interesting than Matthias (it is not a recast!). The star of the story is not the church that Matthias administers but the God who acts in and for the world. Acts is a story about the God who brings salvation to the world through Jesus Christ. The stars of this story are God and the world.

The church is the community that believes it is not the star of its own story. This belief comes back to dying in humility. Theologians use the Greek work *kenōsis* to describe this kind of death. In Philippians 2:6–11, Paul gives us an early hymn of the church that uses the word *kenōsis* to describe how Jesus comes into the world. In verse 7 Jesus empties himself. Paul had earlier pointed to humility in verse 3 and told the church to look after the interests of others, not their own. Paul instructs the church to enter another's story, to empty itself of what it can claim as its own, just like Jesus does. As with Jesus, this emptying, this dying in humility, allows us to enter into the world. The church exists only as it attends to the story of God in the world.

Luke follows Paul, not Matthias. Paul plays his humble part in the larger story of God's action in the world, for the sake of the world's salvation. Paul is central because he goes into the world filled with the Holy Spirit to testify to God's action. Paul finds himself in conflict with the establishment, with Peter and the others in Jerusalem (see Acts 11:2 for a starter), because he centers God's activity among the gentiles. Paul goes into the gentile world to start churches in homes, to wait for God, to retell their own stories of encountering the living Jesus Christ.

Just because the church is not the star does not mean it has no role to play. Best Supporting Actor is an important Oscar category. The church is essential, but only as it realizes and confesses that it is not the star of its own story. The church can be faithful only when its focus is *not* on its own actions but on the acts of God. The story the church is living is not primarily about the church at all! The church lives for a bigger story. The church is called to rehearse and remember, again and again, the stories of God's acts and Jesus's continued life in the very places, the very cities—whether Galatia, Ephesus, Milwaukee, or Toronto—where the church is waiting right now.

Paul starts churches not for the sake of churches, not to stave off decline or accelerate growth, but for the sake of forming communities that serve the world by witnessing to God's acts in the world. For Paul, the setting for God's actions is not the church but the world. Or better, God acts through the church for the sake of the world. The church is the gathered people who are in the world, like Paul, and who have experienced the acts of God through an encounter with Jesus Christ. It is the community that rehearses and narrates the story of God's acts for the world, waiting together for God's coming again in the return of Jesus.

God's act frees us to wait *in Christ*. The waiting that God invites us into is not a dull void but an invitation to participate in God's own life. Not by doing, achieving, and possessing but by waiting attentively on God. It's the gift of having a purpose, even an identity, that has its origin in something other than our anxious selves. Its identity is found in the story and person of Jesus Christ.

## Mixed-Up Stories

You might be thinking, these are nice theological ideas, but they seem disconnected from the decisions we need to make for our congregation. We can't wait. If we wait, we'll be closed in a few months. If our car idles here any longer, it might start rusting. We understand the sentiment. Yet, this is exactly where things get mixed up. We seem so anxious that it confuses us about who is the star of the church's story. Inside the anxiety and anger, we become obsessed with our own story. Anxious for the church, we make the church the star of its story. The church, and particularly the local congregation we care about, is all that matters. After all, we joined the council, leadership team, or session because we wanted to make sure this congregation survived. The most important thing, the very thing I should focus my attention on, is First Church of Somewhere's survival. That's what matters! That's why I'm reading this book!

Our attention is laser-focused on the church for good reasons. We're obsessed with making the church the star of its own story not because we're narcissists but because we're anxious. We fear that the church—the congregation we love—is going to miss out on the good things ahead. It's about to lose funding, new members, and so much more. We remember decades ago when this congregation wasn't so fragile, everything so much less tenuous. Even young churches remember how much easier it was to plant a church with large denomination support in a largely Christendom world. But now, if something isn't done (by us!), we'll be out in the cold. If we don't focus intently on the church, if we don't become obsessed with the congregation's actions, we'll lose our building and our pastor. If we don't make our congregation the star of its own story and get moving faster and faster, we'll be left with only memories and regrets.

Inside this anxiety it seems only right, even faithful and responsible, to give all our attention to the acts of the church. We need to *do* something and fast! We need solutions! Inside the anxiety to do something fast, waiting is a distasteful enemy. Ultimately, this anxiety confuses us.

But waiting is our friend. The only way we can survive is by waiting. Waiting puts our attention in the right place. When we forget to wait, we become too distracted, too impatient, too angry to see God's action. The stories that form the church are about God's actions. Attention ought not to be on the church but on the God who moves, the Jesus who lives, bringing life out of death. The church is the witness, the narrator, to the bigger story of God's action to save the world.

We know of very few churches that intentionally turn away from God. They don't do it on purpose. It happens because our attention is directed somewhere else and our secular imaginations don't let us see that. With our attention on the anxiety to survive and the rush to do something, God is inevitably replaced as the star of the church's story. It becomes so easy, particularly in our secular age, for God to be just a subplot of our congregational life. We're so anxious that this becomes inevitable.

We can see some of your eyes rolling. Some of you may be scoffing at such pious statements about God. A few of you may even be choking on the abstraction. You're thinking, "Right, this is all easy for you to say, but we have a leaking roof and an $80,000 deficit in our budget." Or, "Sure, I love God, but we're hemorrhaging members and can't fill our open position for a pastor." And you might add, "Look around. Churches are closing, our denomination is laying off staff, and we're reading about studies that show fewer and fewer people are going to church. It's bleak!"

It's true, these are hard times for congregations because we are living in a difficult moment for the church. The twenty-first century has been a struggle for congregations. We're not denying that. No Pollyanna here. But let's have some perspective—that's hard when you're anxious. There have been *much more* difficult times for the church than the one we're living through now. And the church survived. There have been periods of living under hostile political regimes (such as twentieth-century China), times of deep corruption (such as during the Borgias popes), situations of vicious division (such as the Thirty Years' War). The church has lived through many periods of crisis. So let's be faithful stewards—realistic, but not catastrophizing. A society-wide crisis such as oppression, corruption, and division takes our attention away from the fact that the church of Jesus Christ is created and sustained by Jesus Christ. From our vantage, the secular age that leads to acceleration is just a crisis, taking our attention away from the story of God and putting it squarely on the crisis of decline.

With Paul and the saints of the past, we believe that no power, principality, budget shortfall, or leaking roof can stop God from acting. The church is the body of the resurrected Christ, and no body can ignore its head and expect to get anywhere. The

Holy Spirit, who creates, accompanies, and sustains the church through the life, death, resurrection, ascension, and promised return of Jesus Christ, commands the church to wait. The church has its life in *being* together, experiencing the Spirit leading us into the world to love the world. We're commanded to wait even in these hard times.

## The Crisis of Decline

Let's be honest and specific. It's ultimately the *decline* that makes us anxious. The decline shapes the crisis. This crisis of decline and its anxiety makes us obsessed with the church being the star of its own story. It leads us to assume there is no other option. The crisis the church faces isn't fundamentally one of oppression, corruption, or division. No, the popular story goes, the crisis the twenty-first-century church faces is decline. The anxiety brought on by this decline leads us to tell all sorts of stories about the church that push the church into the spotlight. We feel stuck on a parkway about to miss all the good things waiting for us at the end of the trip because we must wait, thanks to the decline of resources and relevance. Feeling the hot breath of decline, waiting seems to be a repulsive enemy. Yet, we have learned from other crises the church has faced in its history that the only way out is *not* to focus on the church but instead to return our attention to the God who acts.

Consultants counsel declining congregations all the time to own their story. If a congregation is to survive and thrive—which really means *compete*—it is essential that it find its own unique assets, so they say. The congregation must discover its own story, which usually means something like its brand. The congregation must hire a dynamic leader so it can win some ground in the declining religious market. The issue for most congregations, it's assumed, is that they've lost *their* own story. When they've lost their story, they've lost the drive to innovate and compete for success. The consultant reminds us that when we know our story, we know how to act. Know your why. The thought is that the congregation has lost what makes it different and unique, ready to act.

But for what purpose are those actions done? For winning resources and relevance that will beat back decline. In a competitive religious marketplace—competitive because it's such a shrinking market—there is no patience for waiting. "Fortune favors the brave," as Matt Damon told us over and over again in a very annoying commercial for cryptocurrency in fall of 2021. Fortune favors those who do not wait, for those who have their own story and act in and for that story, which they are the star of. But Jesus tells the church in Acts 1 that it has no story other than Jesus's own.

The part Jesus does command the church to play in *his* story is to wait. Wait so that the Spirit can lead the church in following Christ in the world. When we feel the anxiety of decline, waiting becomes our enemy and we seek to make ourselves (our own competing congregation) the star of our own story.

But we get it! This all is very hard when we assume we're in crisis.

Maybe it's true. Maybe we are in crisis.

But maybe the crisis isn't what we think it is.

# 5

# Waiting Brings Life,
# Not a Slow Death

We both have teenaged children. Between the two of us, we have
five teenagers (we could use your prayers!). For all of our kids,
technology is in the air they breathe. They move so effortlessly
inside digital spaces. Their whole lives they've had an almost
sixth sense on how to use tablets, apps, and other technology. It
amazes us, as we watch them, how smooth it all is. It all works!
Our children know only a world where technology works just
as it's advertised.

We both grew up in the late 1980s and 1990s (Blair is older
than Andy by two years, but those are Canadian years, which
is like eight American years!). We came of age during the first
wave of the microprocessor revolution. We were the first generation to have home video game consoles (Atari 2600 and NES!),
programmable VCRs, and electronic daytimers such as the Palm

Pilot. It was amazing. But never, ever smooth. Those early arrivals of our coming technological age were always clunky and almost never worked as promised. It was glitch on top of glitch. You could never count on all the advertised features to work. For instance, the VCR could almost always play a tape, but programming it to record a show almost never worked. And you needed ten years of engineering experience at NASA to figure out how to set the clock. Most families just let it blink "12:00" "12:00" "12:00" continually.

Everything now is smooth. We love smooth. We expect smooth. We need smooth to the point where frustration, conflict, and negativity become debilitating. We see it with our children. They're so savvy and creative, but resilience, or even a stomach for tension and conflict, is another matter.

## A Church in Conflict

We often hear a similar frustration with the church. We just want it to be smooth. We're frustrated because it's so glitchy. It's not working as promised (although, if we are being honest, we carry the promises of our own consumer expectations, not the promises of God). The anxiety frustrates us. Or maybe it's the frustration that makes us anxious. Regardless, we just want it to be smooth. Is that so much to ask? We can't wait. We hate the idea of waiting, because it means we must accept tension, uncertainty, and vulnerability. Waiting means we have to live with the glitches. When things aren't smooth, sitting and embracing the tension as waiting seems disgusting. What sane person, in a society obsessed with smooth, wants to make their home in a crisis?

Yet, we need to realize that tension, even crisis, is deep in the DNA of the church. To obey Jesus's command—to be the body of the living Christ—the church will *always* be in tension. There will always be some level of discord, some crisis.

Inside our obsession with smooth, we think tension, discord, and crisis will kill us. It's what's killing the church, we assume. But actually, it's the opposite. Tension, discord, and even crisis, though uncomfortable, are signs of life. Life always comes amid tension, discord, and crisis. The birth of any mammal is an example. Of course, tension, discord, and crisis can spin out into dysfunction, destruction, and dehumanization. But often the three terrible D's arrive when we try to smother, shame, and shun those we believe are responsible for interrupting our smooth with tension. Earlier we mentioned Mars Hill Church in Seattle. The deep abuses that happen in churches like that often start with leaders who want to move quickly, seeing the smooth as essential for growth, so they have no patience for tension and no desire to accept living with discord. Instead, they demand everyone do their part in keeping things smooth, so the church (Or is it the pastor's platform? Is there a difference in a megachurch?) can grow.

But this problem isn't exclusive to tabloid celebrity churches. It's us too. We want to act quickly, making the congregation the star of its own story, because we want to solve the crisis of decline and get things back to the smooth. To solve the crisis of decline we need to eliminate glitches and do away with tensions. The pastor imagines that this is their job. We all assume, in a logic not that different from that of the celebrity churches, that if we only have *more* (more members, more dollars, more relevance, more resources, all of those things helping to procure more of the others), we could call an end to the crisis. The crisis days would be over and gone! (Cue the 1920s song "Happy Days Are Here Again.") We could put away for good all the tensions, discord, and crises and slide into smooth sailing.

## Two Mistakes

### *1. No Tension = No Community*

It is a mistake to assume that a community of faith, your congregation, could ever live without tension, discord, and even conflict. It can't if the church wants to be alive. Dietrich Bonhoeffer—the pastor and theologian who was murdered by Hitler in the last days of World War II—in his famous little book *Life Together* is clear that to love the church is to love the real church.

There is a great temptation to love the idea of community, to even love the ideal church. But there is no such thing. Maybe there would be if God were just an idea. But God can never be assumed to be an idea because God has made Godself known in the person of Jesus Christ. Jesus is no idea, but a person. Jesus is God incarnate, embodied, bearing all the tensions and discords of life. Because the church is the body of the embodied God, there can be no ideal church. Just the real community of the real bodies of real persons in real relationship. There can be no perfectly smooth (even mostly smooth) congregation. To try to live beyond tensions is to photoshop the body of the church, taking out all the acne and replacing it with plastic-looking skin. To do so is to worship the fake over the real, brand over community. To want a church without tension, discord, and conflict is to confuse the fake for the real.

Real communities, made up of real people living real lives, are always in tension. Bonhoeffer frequently draws parallels to families. He reminds us that good families (not ideal ones) that are living together and loving one another are always moving in and out of conflict and tension. Family life, at its best, is full and meaningful, but never, ever smooth. Siblings who love each other deeply, happily giving a kidney for the other, are always moving in and out of conflict and tension. Often, the closer they are, the more they fight. Road-trip tensions seem to follow or lead right into moments of intimacy. These tensions and flows of discord are a sign of health and love. We rightfully fear and distrust the perfectly smooth family. The robot-like family with no tensions and no conflicts is frightening. Such families make for a creepy horror movie. They are perfectly smooth but not alive.

Bonhoeffer's point is that to love the church is to love the real church made up of real people. We can end the tensions and discord in the church only if we pretend the church is not made up of real people with real bodies. We can get there only if we photoshop everything smooth, covering up our scars and tears, smoothing away the wrinkles from our laughter and joy. A church that can't wait can't embrace tensions and discord. And a church that can't embrace tensions and discord, making a way even in conflict, is a church that may look smooth but is not alive.

### 2. No Crisis = No God

The second mistake assumes that the theme song for the church could ever be "Happy Days Are Here Again." We admit it's not cool to refer to a song from 1929 (remember, Blair isn't cool, so a bit of grace there). It is an *old* song, but you may have heard it. It's catchy. Like a good Bruce Springsteen or Nirvana song, it captures the spirit of its time. It's soaked in its *zeitgeist*, so much so that the song was used as the theme of Franklin D. Roosevelt's 1932 presidential campaign. It was perfect. The song encompassed in spirit as well as message that the crisis was *over*. The Great Depression was behind us! The crisis of decline had ended! Prosperity was back! Smooth, happy days were here again. Thanks to FDR, crisis would be buried for good (at least until Pearl Harbor was set ablaze—but that's not our point).

Those of us on church boards, councils, and sessions want so badly to roll that song. We want to bring happy days back again to our church. We'd all love to do a carefree jig through a full Sunday school wing, singing about happy days returning. We long to bury decline forever and find a way back to prosperity. But not like the prosperity of TV evangelists. Not *that* kind of prosperity. Just a surplus of resources and relevance to keep our congregation safely out of the crisis zone. Prosperity would be great, but ultimately what we really want is to secure the church beyond crisis. To return to days when our congregation wasn't so fragile. That's not a bad ambition. We could all use less fragility, or what economists call "precarity." Moving people from a precarious to a stable situation is a laudable goal. But we should be careful. This desire to be less fragile should not be *at the expense of crisis*. We need crisis! There is no way outside crisis.

I bet your response to those last few sentences was, "Huh?" Let us explain.

If we're not careful, the desire to eliminate decline tempts us with the smooth. There is no way for the church to be the church without crisis. The church must be possessed by crisis because the church is a child of crisis. Crisis itself isn't a cancerous tumor to cut out. The church before the return of Christ will, by necessity, always be living with and out of crisis. Crisis is the very organ—the heart—of the church itself. To mistake the crisis for cancer is to risk cutting out the source of life from the church. Sure, it would be nice for our congregation to be less fragile. But this shouldn't lead us to the mistake of believing we can live outside crisis—sipping umbrella drinks forevermore.

The church will never be called to an easy-street, crisis-free life. The fact that we think the church could *be* beyond crisis, seeing crisis as a tumor and not a vital organ, reveals that we're all mixed up on what this crisis is all about. This confusion may be the real source of our issues.

We too often think that the crisis could be ended, and church could be beyond crisis, because we assume the crisis is *decline*. With this assumption, we seek ways to get back to the smooth, to secure prosperity, and to end all tensions and conflicts forever in happy days. That's a Disney fantasy that has no connection to the God of the Bible, no relation to the church in Acts 1. The church in the first few chapters of Acts, and our own congregations, can only have life by *being* inside a crisis. By being possessed by crisis. By making our home inside crisis. It's only inside a crisis that the church can faithfully be the church.

We want to sit with this talk of crisis, because it is so important to know it in our gut. We believe that the problem with most Protestant congregations is that they've misidentified the crisis. We've had no stomach for crisis, partly because this is what our secular age does to us and partly because we've focused, almost completely, on the wrong crisis. Our attention has been almost completely on the crisis of decline. But the crisis we should be focused on—the crisis that is the heart of the church and not a tumor—is a crisis we can never escape and still be the church of Jesus Christ. This crisis is weird, even mystical. It's the kind of crisis that doesn't ask us to do more, to *hurry* and to *have* as a way of stabilizing ourselves. This crisis is different. The only way to live in this crisis is to wait. Jesus commands us in Acts 1 to wait inside this crisis. This crisis demands attentive waiting, that we try to see and hear what's so easily blurred in our secular age.

To finally name it: the real crisis is encountering a living God who is God. God is real. God is God, and we are not. To encounter this real God as humans constitutes a crisis. We've become so focused on the crisis of decline that we deny or push aside the crisis that we are broken and sinful people, a weak church, who are called to wait for the God who is God to act in our midst. We come to think that waiting for a God who is God to act in the world is not a crisis worth our attention. We come to believe that the crisis of encounter with this living God is not something worth capturing our attention. This misguided assumption is the real cancer!

When we ignore the crisis of God's action and conclude that the crisis is decline, we attack crisis itself. We have dreams of living beyond crisis, ending crisis for a smoother life. We deny that we are in need of God's action to save us. Instead, we take action to save ourselves. We seek to dilute the taste of crisis with buckets and buckets of overflowing relevance and resources. While these overflowing buckets may dull our sense of crisis, they will never end it. They will never end crisis because the crisis the church faces, and must never live without, cannot be ended.

Human beings will always have their attention on some crisis. Because we're creatures who feel, putting those feelings into stories, what we hold to be a primary crisis will (and should) always dominate and monopolize our attention. Everything we feel and know should be colored by the primary or central crisis that possesses us. Our breath should take the rhythm of the crisis we're staring down. To be human is to be possessed by something, by some crisis.

It becomes a major problem to have our attention on—to be possessed by—the wrong crisis. If the crisis we face will indelibly shape our lives, it would be a shame, a deep waste, and a major malformation, even a disobedience, to be possessed by the wrong crisis. Decline may have its challenges, but it is the *wrong* crisis. Our attention should be on the crisis of God's own action. How do we discern God's action? How do we help our people experience, know, and follow this living God who acts? This living God who is beyond and greater than all experience and all knowing? That is the crisis. We should be tossing and turning, asking, How can we help our people encounter the living God in a secular age that blinds them to anything beyond the here and now?

The church *is* inside the crisis of God's living action in the world. This is why Jesus calls us to wait in Acts 1, to wait for this action and the Spirit to discern it. In our waiting, the right crisis might shape us, bringing our attention to the living God. Waiting inside this crisis makes waiting itself anything but meaningless boredom, anything but do-nothingism. The crisis of God's action is the crisis that does something paradoxical. Waiting inside this crisis, waiting for God's action, leaning further into this crisis, doesn't undo the church but makes and sustains the church. This waiting even sends the church into the world to wait with the world for God's action to save the world. *This* crisis gives life. This crisis is the blood that runs through the church's veins.

## A Danish Treat and the God Who Is Crisis

Think back to those encounters along the road, the one to Emmaus and the one to Damascus. The disciples in Luke 24 are sitting at the table. They feel the absence of Jesus, but he is right there in front of them. When he breaks the bread, their eyes open and their hearts are strangely warmed. Then they return to Jerusalem as witnesses. It is a crisis.

In Acts 9, when Jesus comes to Saul, he chooses Saul as God's apostle. It interrupts all that Saul knows, taking him through a death and giving him a new life. Saul comes to recognize that this Jesus is true God of true God. Saul is now inside the crisis of knowing the unknowable. Saul, soon to be Paul, now needs to proclaim as known what cannot be known. It's with this crisis at the center that Paul starts all his churches throughout the story that Luke tells us in the book of Acts. It is a crisis.

We know that all of this is a little mind spinning, and it will only get worse, so how about a little Danish treat to help it go down?

This Danish treat isn't a pastry but a very odd duck. About a hundred years before Dietrich Bonhoeffer was writing *Life Together* and before people were wiggling their shoulders to "Happy Days Are Here Again," an odd young man was making trouble in Denmark. This young man's father was very rich but very unhappy. His father's unhappiness made the father very religious. The father had the crisis all wrong. The father was using religion as a medication, not as an invitation into the crisis of God's life and action. This odd young man had an older brother who was a Lutheran pastor outside Copenhagen. After his studies, the young man, named Søren Kierkegaard, started making trouble. His father's and his brother's religion seemed to overlook something essential.

While Søren was a bother to his father and brother, he was a real pain for Hans Martensen, Denmark's top theology professor and leading bishop. Martensen was the best the church had. Søren decided to take aim. He didn't want to be a pain, but he believed that Martensen had exchanged the gospel of Jesus Christ for the prosperity of the Church of Denmark. Søren believed that, like Esau long ago (Gen. 25:29–34), the Church of Denmark had given up its birthright of crisis for a hot bowl of crisis-free stew.

The Danish population took notice of Søren's writings. Overall, these were happy days for the Danish church, making Søren seem irritable and morose. There was no scent of decline for the Church of Denmark in the mid-nineteenth century, because the church had successfully put it away. The church had more resources and relevance than it needed. Happy days were here for the Church of Denmark!

Those happy days troubled Søren. He forcefully responded that there were *no* Christians—not one Christ follower—in *all* of Denmark! Søren's brilliance always started with hyperbole. But he had a point, and we should listen. To hear Søren tell it, they were all too buffered from crisis to encounter the living God of Jesus Christ. The Danish church had comfortably committed itself to the ideas of its religion that did not include the crisis of God. Its God wasn't a living being but an idea. Religion became a moat, protecting the church from crisis. From Søren's point of view, no crisis means no God.

The Church of Denmark was a church beyond crisis, which assured Søren it was a church of disobedience. It was full and it looked good, but that was just a handsome veneer. A shiny coat to hide an inner vapidness. The Church of Denmark was a church that could make no sense of and therefore had no love for the cross of Jesus Christ (the cross itself revealing that crisis cannot be deleted from God's own life).

Søren believed, from his reading of the Bible, that without crisis you could not know the God who is the God made known in the life of Abraham and most fully known in the cross of Christ. In righteous anger, Søren wrote that the nineteenth-century Danish church grotesquely flipped things. It thought it controlled God, that God served Martensen, not vice versa, that the Church of Denmark was stronger than God. Ultimately, it believed that God was its pet.

But God is God. There is nothing greater, no way to ever capture and control God. Not in our churches, not in our dogmas, not in our liturgies, not even in our shiny, full buildings glowing with prosperity. That's the problem with a church that wants a smooth life beyond crisis. It wants to control God. But God is not smooth. Not a pet. God is wild. And this wild God is not usually known in happy days of self-made prosperity.

The church cannot be without crisis, because the church worships the God who is God. The wild, acting God. In turn, the church confesses that there is no way to know this God who is God. There are no human tactics or technologies, no religious mechanisms that can conjure up this God who is God. And yet God *can* be known. For thousands of years the church has confessed that it knows God. This knowing is possible only because this God who is God chooses to make Godself known to us. We can't conjure up God, but God does promise to make Godself known to us. We can only know God because *God* reveals God.

I know, we're causing your brain to spin like a top. It's really going now, isn't it? Hang in there. Maybe a story or two will help with the nausea (call it story-based Dramamine).

## A Two-Story Interlude

We both do a lot of teaching at churches. We enjoy walking into a church fellowship hall and leading the education hour with a group of learners. Sometimes these groups are intergenerational. Such groups are always challenging but more rewarding. A few years back we did one on faith and science with adults and teenagers. We put the teenagers and adults in groups of five or six around tables. They were asked, with no constraints, to come up with three big questions that they've always wrestled with and share them with the group. Of course, there were questions about evolution, life after death, and whether Adam and Eve were real people. But then an adult, a professional and educated woman in her forties, raised her hand and asked, "I've always wondered, who created God? I mean what was before God and what or who made God?"

We stared back. Listening carefully, we heard Plato, the psalmists, and all the participants who wrote the Nicene Creed roll over in their graves. Maybe we shouldn't have been surprised by the question. A lot of other people were probably thinking it—maybe you have. This was a group of Americans, after all. American education tends to focus more on STEM (science, technology, engineering, and mathematics) and much less on the questions taken up by theology or philosophy. In some parts of the world, small children wrestle with philosophical questions in school, some reading Plato by fifth grade. This woman's question, far from dumb, just showed how easy it is, even in the church, to misunderstand what we mean when we say "God."

Plato and the psalmists long ago taught us that to say "God" is to say "that which there is *nothing* greater than." To say "God" is to say the One who has no beginning and no end. The One who stands completely above and beyond us. The One who is wholly and completely other than all that is. To say "God" is to say the One who is so grand and great that our minds cannot capture even 0.00000000001 percent (maybe add a bunch more zeros) of this God's grand greatness.

It's a crisis, then, to even try and say anything about the One whom we can know so little about. We simply don't possess the cognitive equipment to comprehend God. And yet the church must say something about this great, completely other God.

The woman's question (again, not a bad question) assumed that God was just a bigger, supersized version of us. But that is not the God whom Plato, the Bible, or the church fathers teach us about. The God they speak of is wholly and completely other than us. This God is God, not just all that is good about humans on mega-steroids. The God they teach us about is a God who has no beginning and no end. God comes from nothing else, unmade and unbegotten. That's hard for us to understand because all people (all created things) come from somewhere, begotten and made by some force. God is a force for which there is nothing greater. This sets God apart. All of this is what we mean when we say "God." We mean the One of whom nothing greater can be said. The One who is completely and totally other than us, and other than all that is.

The crisis the church faces is that it worships and serves such a God who is so great, so other, that we cannot say, or even know, anything about this God. And yet—here is the crisis—we nevertheless must speak of and witness to this One who is God. Søren's point is that Martensen and the Church of Denmark became so impressed with their own voice, their own abilities, that they confused themselves with God. They were so impressed with their own thoughts and accomplishments that they began to believe that their sermons, liturgies, and church programs could match the power of, and even control, God. ("What stupid hubris!" Søren shouts.) The Danish church had forgotten that this God is too great to know, too other to even understand. Thinking we know anything about this great God is like asking a six-year-old to lecture on gravity and string theory to a group of Ivy League physics professors. That's a crisis!

I'm sure this crisis feels heavy. Not a great medication to the disequilibrium. But it raises another big issue. If God is so other than us, unpossessable by us, if we're just six-year-olds muttering nonsense, then maybe we should just give up! How can we ever really say anything about this God at all? Perhaps the crisis is so great we should just quit altogether. (No wonder that after Søren died, no one in Denmark named their child Søren for a generation.)

But there is a way forward: lean into the crisis. To see how, let's go even further back in time.

Imagine it's the 1520s. You're a new student at the university in Wittenberg in Germany. You're studying to be a clerk. Your dream is to one day be the secretary for a great house, maybe even the secretary of a prince. Clearly this isn't America. There is no "America." This isn't even a world with a scientific revolution—not yet. Your education will center on theology and philosophy. You're told to take a course in Bible from the Psalms professor. The rumor is that, like Søren, this professor is at times irritable and morose but always brilliantly engaging.

One day in class a question comes to your mind. The professor is on a roll. He's opening your mind by opening the Scriptures. There are rumors that he's opening the minds of all of Europe by opposing the theologians and the bishop of Rome. He's attacking even bigger fish than Martensen. You decide to ask your question. You raise your hand. The sweaty, wild-eyed professor nods at you. You clear your throat and say, "Professor Luther, what was God doing before God created the world?"

This is not the same question as that of the American woman in her forties. This question assumes what the psalmists have taught us—that God is greater and completely other, not dependent on anything. That God is the beginning and the end. It feels like a good question. If God is eternal, what was God doing before there was time?

Professor Luther's eyes get big. He bites his bottom lip, grimaces, and replies through his teeth: "Cutting switches to beat

95

people who ask such questions." The whole class gulps. You decide that's enough question asking for you. If it had happened in the twenty-first century, you might have started composing an email to the dean.

In the twentieth century, Dietrich Bonhoeffer discussed this incident. Bonhoeffer tells this story and says, "Luther wasn't just cutting the student down, but Luther was also making a larger point."[1] And what exactly was that? How could this takedown keep us from wilting under the heat of God's otherness and our own childish babbling? Luther wants the student to know that even though this God is completely other, God has made Godself known to us. We cannot climb to some mental or spiritual location to know God. But God can and does reveal Godself to us.

Luther's burn reminds the student that he is a human being and therefore cannot, should not, concern himself with God outside the ways that God has made Godself known to us. Don't waste your time trying to see behind God; rather, recognize that this God has acted in the world. Focus on the acts of this God—that alone is how you will know this God. We will know this God by waiting and watching for God's action in the world. By reading and telling the stories of God's acting in the Bible. Because we are creatures bound to the world, we can know the true God only as God has made Godself known in (and for) the world.

Good point, Bonhoeffer.

There is yet another dimension to the crisis, and it further reveals why we *must* always be a waiting people, the waiting church. The crisis goes deeper because this God does not reveal Godself on a stadium Jumbotron or by Instagram influencers. God reveals Godself by the way of a woman with a barren womb (Gen. 17:15–16), a stuttering prophet (Exod. 4:10–11), and a poor, pregnant-but-virgin teenager (Luke 1:26–38). Ultimately, God reveals Godself in the crucified Jesus.

Let's admit it: God comes to us in very backward ways. At first glance, these ways are not what we would expect. That's a gift. God comes in these odd ways, in suffering and yearning, so that we know we do not conjure up or control God. Sarah, Moses, Mary, and so many others have no way to overcome their crises. Only when God arrives—meeting them in their waiting and sending them to witness—do they overcome. This coming to us reveals who God is. This God-who-cannot-be-known is known as the God who comes to save and love us. The God who meets Sarah with a barren womb, Moses with a speech impairment, and Mary with a seemingly shameful pregnancy shows that God *is* love.

The depth of the crisis is that the God we know is the God who is God and therefore cannot be known. Unless—unless!—this God reveals Godself to us. We must wait for this revealing! We can be the church of the living God only by waiting for this revealing. And when this God does reveal Godself to us in our waiting, God is revealed in backward, hidden ways that demand the eyes of faith. Faith is the crisis of knowing the true God by how God has revealed Godself in the world. The church has no life other than waiting for and witnessing to the God who reveals Godself in the world in the backward ways of love.

## Back to the Danish

We return to Søren. The Church of Denmark thought it could end all crises and live happily ever after. But to do this, Søren shouted, it would have to make God in its own image. God had to come under its control. Then it would never have to wait for

God to reveal Godself, never be a church in crisis; it could just live smoothly ever after.

The problem is that this God cannot be caged, even in our churches. This God is wild, as we've said. To make this point, Søren reminded the Danish church that there is an incomparable difference between time and eternity. This difference was at the heart of Luther's response to the student. Time and eternity are not different in the way that two breeds of dogs are different. Not even different like apples and oranges. Time and eternity are totally and completely different, with no point of contact between them. Eternity stretches out beyond, while God has created time, setting bounds and limits on it. Eternity can encompass time, can break into time, can fill it. We feel eternity in time in moments of deep connection of love and care. Like when you hold your grandchild, or catch up with an old friend, or serve someone in need. In the Bible, eternity enters time when angels appear (Gen. 18:1–2; Luke 1:26). Or when a bush burns but isn't consumed (Exod. 3:2).

It can't work the other way around. Time cannot enter into eternity without eternity fully enveloping it. Eternity swallows time. Søren's point is that we human beings live on the plane of time, but God is eternal. Time makes up our being while eternity makes up God's. There can be no confusing us for God or God for an object that human beings can control. God is not a created object in time; God orders all time. We cannot, and never will be able to, escape crisis, for we are in time. Time—its ticking, our aging—will always be a crisis for us.

Søren wants us to see that the church, bound in time, made up of time-bound people in tensions and discords, nevertheless is part of the life of the eternal God. We are waiting in time for the eternal God to speak to us, to direct us, to lead us out in service to the world. To ignore this crisis, to assume the crisis is just one of resources and relevance, is to lose who God actually is. Solving the crisis of decline can give you religion, but it will keep your church from waiting on the encounter of the living God who is God.

The church is called to wait because it is alive *only* inside the crisis of God's own life. The crisis that it encounters and participates in is the life of the living God who cannot be known. This God can never be made smooth and controllable. This God is wild. God's actions in the world make it so that the church must always live in the tension of the confession that its life is only in knowing a God it cannot know. The church worships and follows this wild God into the world. The church can never be outside crisis because the God of Israel, the God who raises Jesus from the dead, is uncontrollable. This God cannot be programmed and possessed. The church confesses a paradox that the God who is as tender as a mother's embrace, as close as our own breath, is beyond and other, outside and unknowable. The church can never be the star of its own story, because the God who makes the church can never be caged or captured by the church. Our crisis is continual because God is God. Because God is God, we must wait.

# 6

# Forget the Mission
# Statement—Get a Watchword

It all started in the 1980s. The landscape of business was changing. Before the 1980s, businesses were either slow giants or small
ants. There were big corporations like IBM. They had figured
out decades earlier what they were about and what they were
for. There was no reason to rethink it or even question their
purpose. Because these corporations were slow giants, people
swerved out of their way. These businesses didn't need agility,
dexterity, or even reflexes. They just stomped their way forward.

And then there were the ants. These family-owned businesses, such as the small-town grocery or hardware store, didn't
need to think much about agility or dexterity. After all, they
were just ants. Too small for the giants to crush, too close to
the ground, too embedded in their own communities to think
much about why they existed.

But this all changed in the 1980s and into the 1990s. Changes in the economy slayed giants and ate ants. Big corporations found that little garage-based start-ups could stagger them. IBM took it on all sides, Microsoft from within and Apple without. Little family-owned businesses got eaten by corporate chains, such as Walmart. Ma-and-pa stores left community after community.

One lesson became clear. Whether you were a giant or an ant (or even a church), you had better know why you exist. And you had better recheck that *why* often, being flexible and agile, or you would die. You'd have no future. You'd have no way to accelerate, procure resources, and grow. Starting in the mid-1980s, it didn't matter whether you were a giant or an ant (or a church), you needed to grow (and fast). And to grow you needed one thing: a mission statement.

## Where the Mission Statement Comes From

We've already questioned this logic of acceleration and growth. The secular age hitches purpose to acceleration and blocks out transcendence, leaving us stuck with a spiritual depression. We've already pointed that out. But we mention the changes in the '80s because they lead everyone, from businesses to churches, to think that a necessary strategy for staving off decline is a good mission statement.

Every church we know has a mission statement. The logic is simple and taken directly from business: money follows mission. The mission statement keeps giants from being too slow and ants from being too small. They direct everyone's attention and activity, unifying them toward a certain future. Your mission (and its constant revision, or at least the strategic plans that support it) gives direction and steers your agile and flexible response to the future.

We question this logic, but we're not naive. We understand that some of this is necessary. After all, some of you might be thinking, isn't "mission" a theological word? Or at least couldn't it go in that direction? Shouldn't the church be missional?

We think so. But a mission statement and good missional theology are not the same thing. A mission statement is an agreement about how a group of people will direct their actions. It puts our human actions at the center. Missional theology puts the emphasis on God's own action. God is the agent in missional theology. In missional theology, human beings wait and witness, even wait as a form of witness. Mission statements don't lead to waiting. Quite the opposite. They exist so the business or church does not wait, because they assume waiting is wasting.

We've led churches and initiatives. We've launched capital campaigns and overseen grant money in the millions of dollars. We know that in a church under the influence of the secular age, money does follow mission. A mission statement is necessary. But because we've led capital campaigns and million-dollar grant projects, we know that mission statements alone will only enforce immanence, acceleration, and burnout. It's no wonder that since the 1980s the stress level of workers has continued to escalate and burnout has become common.

We think the problem for the church is when the mission statement is not paired with a watchword. Almost every board, council, and session believes its job is to help its congregation live out its mission statement. It at least knows what a mission statement is. Almost none, however, know what a watchword is. We think the watchword—not the mission statement—needs to feed the church community.

The watchword is the foundation that the waiting church builds on. A building takes its shape above ground by what goes on underground. Pour millions of dollars into a fancy church that does not have a good foundation and you will find nothing but grief. In doing a few building projects, we were always amazed by how much money went into site works and the foundation. What a pain, though. It's a hard sell to excite donors about the foundation, because you cannot see it when the building is done. No one wants to leave the foundation of a building as their legacy. Where would you put the plaque saying "The So-and-So Foundation"?

It is not entirely true that you do not see the foundation when the building is done; you just have to look for it. The whole shape of the building comes from the foundation. The walls and roof draw the eye away from the fact that they sit on something that gives them shape and support. This is like the watchword. The church rests on it, but it is hard to see unless you look for it.

"But hold on," we can hear you thinking, "what is a watchword?"

## The Watchword

The church doesn't use "watchword" much anymore. That's good for us, because it helps the church meet the word anew and therefore see its depth. We don't need to fight against preconceived assumptions. Assumptions, as popular sayings remind us, make a fool out of you and me. Too many people think they know what they mean when they say "Jesus Christ is Lord" (hint: this statement "Jesus Christ is Lord" is itself a watchword). The mystery and power of the claim is lost. When everyone thinks they know what these words mean, we forgot just how strange they are. But a watchword helps.

The concept of a watchword has its origins in the fourteenth century and was used often in the eighteenth century. It is a phrase or even a slogan that encompasses a much larger story. It's shorthand for a story of a deep experience that has shaped a group of people. The person with the watchword is called to watch with that word, to look at the world and interact with the world in and through this shorthand story.

In the fourteenth century a watchword was often used like a password. The person on watch would meet the world with the watchword, discerning who was friend or foe by their relation to the word. If someone knew the word, they knew the story. If they knew the story, it was assumed, they had come under its claims. The story had shaped their life, leading them to see things in a certain way.

But the password analogy falls a bit short, because we use passwords to keep people out, to protect what is private, personal, valuable, and therefore needs guarding. Not so much with a watchword. A watchword isn't there to keep things out but to direct our attention. A watchword, like a password, is secretive but for a different reason. The story it tells is a mystery. It is a way of seeing and being that touches the transcendent. A password has no mystery, no inner life that can shape you. Knowing the password can give you access to a bank account, for instance, but it doesn't call you deeper into the meaning of life and why it is worth living. You go right through a password, and it leaves no mark on your life. If the software is written right, you don't even notice the security wall you've passed through. A password is just a lock. A password is completely functional in that way. Its job is to keep the wrong people out, not to shape you. A password is as mysterious and beautiful, shaping your life, as a double-bolted metal door.

A watchword, on the other hand, is different. The watchword, unlike a password, holds a mystery within. A watchword forms you. It's a shorthand story of beauty and encounter. It's shorthand for your shared experience with the living God. You don't pass through a watchword. You take it on, like a pair of glasses, moving in and through the world with a new lens. You use the watchword's narrative shape (not its code) as a way of making sense of the world and your own life in it.

A password almost never shapes your life. IT folks tell us never to generate a password from part of your life. Never use your dog's name or the street you grew up on. But a watchword becomes part of you. It forms you, finding itself next to the most essential parts of your life. A watchword, because it's a story, has a way of shaping your life, while a password is almost completely functional and mathematical.

A watchword's job is not to keep out but to form and mold those within. The watchword is the lens through which we look out into the world for the living God. The watchword is how we cope with the crisis of a living God who acts. It helps us discern the ways this living God who is God acts in the world. The watchword is a story or slogan of how this church, this community, has encountered the living God.

## Kitchen Table Watchwords

In a waiting church, we find our watchword and then help our people live it out. Our waiting isn't a dull inaction but an attentiveness, and the watchword is what shapes that attention. With the watchword, we go out into the world to wait for the acting God. We're formed, changed, and transformed as we enter the world with the watchword because it gives us a new story to live out of. It gives us a way of seeing and being in the world. We can't ask the people in our congregation to wait for God without shaping their waiting.

One of the best illustrations of a watchword comes from the early days of the civil rights movement. It's January 27, 1956. Martin Luther King Jr. is in his second year as pastor of Dexter Avenue Baptist Church in Montgomery, Alabama.[1] He's been picked to help lead the bus boycotts. Things are not going well. King is pushing his people to *do* more. But the strong headwinds are creating little progress. And now the threats are becoming vicious. Late on January 27, the phone in King's house rings. With his wife and infant child asleep, King answers it to hear, "N——, we're tired of your mess. And if you aren't out of this town in three days, we're going to blow up your house and blow your brains out."

Though not the first threat on King's life, this one shakes him. Maybe it's because of his baby sleeping soundly in the next room. Or maybe it's because the boycott is going poorly. King has a mission statement, something like bringing forth equity and civil rights. But that isn't enough. He needs a watchword. King sits at his kitchen table and prays. He confesses to God that his own action is failing, that he has no power to meet his mission. King cries out to God, "Lord, I'm down here trying to do what's right. . . . But I am afraid. . . . I must confess . . . I'm losing my courage." In the moment of that confession, King hears God speak to him, telling him to stand up, that God will be his strength. King hears God say to him, "When there is no way, I'll make a way."

This became King's, and by extension the civil rights movement's, watchword. Through King's leadership, the movement went into the world to wait (at the front of buses, at diner counters) with the mission of bringing forth civil rights. But the mission was possible only because they were formed by the watchword. They waited—their waiting an action—because they knew that out of no way, God makes a way. When things

seemed impossible, when there seemed to be no way, they together became more attentive, anticipating and even preparing
for the God of the exodus to act. The watchword shaped and
readied them to see and respond to God's action in the world.

There is no doubt that people need a mission (we all need
purpose). But this mission, or purpose-driven-ness, must be con-
ditioned by a watchword—by a story or slogan of the God who
is God acting. We believe that the board, council, and session
should oversee a congregation's mission. But more importantly,
they need to help the congregation find its watchword. Then they
need to lead, mainly by repeating, rehearsing, and retelling the
watchword. Reminding the congregation to be attentive, by use
of the watchword, waiting for the living God to act in their lives
and in the congregation as in the world.

## Finding the Watchword

Because a watchword cannot be bought, copied, or manufac-
tured (which is a problem in a world that can buy, copy, or make
a solution to every problem), leaders need to lead. You can't just
go to a conference or read a book (not even this one!) and come
home with a watchword. It must be found by your community.
A watchword is unique to each community of faith because it
is born out of the way this people, in this time and place, have
encountered God's action in the world. The watchword is the
shorthand story of how these people in this moment have witnessed and encountered the living God in the world.

We think there are two very basic moves that churches can
do that will help in finding a watchword. The first is to learn
how to encounter each other. The secular age of acceleration
means that we do not actually see or hear each other as people
but as tools on the way to getting more. The second is that we

need to wait in the right way so that we can encounter God. By causing us to fix our attention on the immanent, the secular age we live in makes it hard to imagine a God who is God, beyond but knowable.

Both of these steps center on storytelling, something everyone loves even if they believe they are not good at it. The first step asks, Where do I see God in my life and in the life of the people around me? In my life, and in the life of the people I encounter, how is God a character in that story? The second asks, Where do we see God working in our midst for the salvation of the world? God is at work in the world, and when we pay attention we might see that.

The board, council, and session's leadership begins by listening for stories. It creates a place where all people feel invited to share their stories of God's presence and absence. Leaders create spaces for people to speak of the ways they see God moving in the world, of stories where they've felt called to minister or to be ministered to. To tell of those times when they cared for a hurting coworker or drove a friend to chemo appointments or any of the other myriad of ways in which we see and hear each other and the world in all of our pain and glory.

Churches find their watchword when they discern a theme in these stories. There is a narrative red thread, divinely woven into and linking all of these stories. When we share deep experiences of God, we pass that on. It becomes a watchword when it becomes a way of discernment. In returning to Acts and seeing how the early church actually got its start, we have had to look at Paul, really the twelfth apostle. The church knows Paul as one of the first theologians but not because he has degrees and a university chair. His authority rests on his encounter with the living Jesus, who sent him into the world with the watchword of the cross. Paul sees the world through the cross. He gathers people to hear his story, one that centers the cross. In hearing his story, the watchword becomes their own, shaped anew by their own encounters with this same living God. Paul's watchword is something like, "I decided to know nothing among you except Jesus Christ, and him crucified" (1 Cor. 2:2). This phrase holds a story of encounter that reveals both a way of life and the path to God.

Almost all doctrines have their origins as watchwords of a particular community. Not all watchwords become doctrines, but all doctrines were watchwords. Martin Luther was a master of watchwords. The Reformation transformed society because it gave people shorthand slogans of deep stories of God's action. "Justification by faith alone," "the theology of the cross," and "*simul Justus et Peccator*" ("at once justified and sinner," or in a looser translation "sinner and saint at the same time") are all shorthand for the ways God acts in the world. They all grew out of Luther's experience of encountering the living God. They are slogans, watchwords, that have spread beyond one congregation, becoming trusted ways by which the God who is God acts in the world.

Of course, we all know—particularly us living in a hyperconsumeristic society—that slogans can become flat. Too often, slogans are just marketing, a seductive way of manipulating people. This happens when the slogan has been disconnected from the stories of our lives, disconnected from the people who encounter the living God. The slogan is flat and stupid, the doctrine banal, when it becomes disconnected from the watchword, when it becomes just a brand.

Many boards, councils, and sessions ask us about branding. They tend to believe that the problem is lack of marketing. "If young adults only knew about us, they'd come," they assume. If they knew our *why*, they would get excited and want to attend, become part of our more. To us, this is the wrong focus. What people want, young adults maybe more than others, what they long for, is not a brand but a watchword to shape their lives, making them attentive to something bigger than themselves. Something that calls out to us. As our teacher Kenda Creasy Dean says, "Unless it is worth dying for, it is not worth living for." No one would die for a brand. But to live for a God who comes to us, saves us, loves us? That seems worthwhile.

## The First Move: Learn to Encounter

The first part of this book discussed how the secular age, the acceleration of time, and the fallout from that make it very difficult for North Americans to actually encounter each other. By "encounter," we mean when two people really see and hear each other. There are limits to our ability to encounter, some practical and some ethical. Practically, we cannot see the entirety of a person because we move through time. We change, and therefore what we see now is not what we will see in the future. As well, there is a great deal to each of us, too much to see all at once. Humans are complex; the stories twist and turn with many subplots. But just because we cannot see all of another person does not mean we can't see enough.

There are ethical limits as well. To remain a distinct person, we all need boundaries. Trust us when we say, you do not want to see us naked. In the metaphor of seeing another person, clothing acts as a kind of limit. It reveals but also conceals, a necessary part of being human. To force someone to get naked, to see them fully, violates their boundaries. This is truer when power enters into the relationship. If one person is playing by the logic of the secular age, they want to consume the other person. We talked about how this plays out in certain church dynamics, especially regarding abuse.

Practical and ethical limits help people know how to have a true, healthy encounter with another person. Many of us have had such encounters. We treasure them because they made us feel whole and understood and valued. Sometimes they happen in a long-term relationship. Consider your favorite teacher growing up. Why did you like that teacher so much? They saw and heard you. To really encounter someone, though, is to see and hear *and* to be seen and heard. There is a back-and-forth in encounter that some relationships resist. The role of teacher and student, especially when the teacher is an adult and the student a child, makes it hard to move to mutuality. The student cannot see or hear the teacher because the teacher must limit themselves. The role prevents a deep encounter, even as the student might feel truly seen and heard. Adult teachers and students have a better chance to see and hear each other. Even there, though, the limit of role and power makes true mutuality nearly impossible.

These limits and complexities of encounter should not discourage us from trying. Think back to Aziz Ansari and his humble death leading to confession. That is a kind of hearing. It was momentary and had all kinds of limits, but it was nonetheless profound. Or George and his laughter. That is a kind of seeing. He was seen by many as useless and slow, but if we open our eyes, we might see him as joyful and present. Again, there are all kinds of limits to this story, but it still has something to show us. Like learning a language that has almost gone extinct, our efforts at encounter will fail and falter, but they will nevertheless be moving us toward the goal of truly connecting with each other. We can and do get it right, and we really do encounter each other.

## The First Move: An Experiment in Encountering One Another

For the past couple of years, we have been working with congregations and ministries to conduct experiments in encounter. COVID both messed up our plan and made the results that much richer. The project helps participants recognize how the secular age shapes their imagination and, in response, empowers them to do small actions that might help them see the world differently. We focus on encounter with the hope that if we can really see and hear each other, we might see and hear God. We launched them into an experiment that took them out of their comfort zone. After that, they came up with their own experiments, using their experience as inspiration.

Our common experiment was part of a larger project based in the UK. Our folks had a chance to engage in PEEL, a project that empowers young people to explore their identity through poetry and photography.[2] That might sound artsy-fartsy. It kind of is. But it is powerful. In PEEL, young people spend five days interviewing one another, really hearing about who their partner is, and then distilling it into a poem and a portrait of that person. They look at the other person through the lens of a professional-grade camera, taking a portrait that sees the other person for who they are. A poet and photographer help, and the results can take your breath away. In a world of throw-away texts and selfies, PEEL teaches young people to hear and see each other. Because they get placed with a partner, there is true mutuality. Both become more human, more real, more themselves, and you can see that in the poems and portraits. They encounter each other.

The congregations and ministries involved in our project participated in a form of PEEL customized for them. Instead of

five days it was three. People of all ages could come. One pair
had a teen and an octogenarian, and by the end, neither would
have had it any other way. Each group had its own reveal, but
everyone came together for a show mounted at a small community gallery attached to a church.[3] Some loved their portrait
so much that it now hangs in their home. A few of the churches
decided to hang the portraits in their narthex or foyer so that
others can encounter people in their community. All participants got a book that included their portraits and poems. Participants reported that they encountered their partner, they felt
more connected to their congregation or ministry, and they were
moved by this profound experience.

This sense of encounter and connection might have been due
to the COVID isolation at the time. People were hungry to be
with each other. For some, PEEL was their first time being with
other people in two years. Already dicey social skills had atro-
phied through endless Zoom meetings. But because they had
tasks with one other person, it was manageable. For instance, we
gave them a list of questions to use in interviewing their partner.
They didn't need to think of how to do it; they just needed to hear
what their partner said. Likewise, a professional photographer
guided them so they didn't need to worry about the complex settings on the camera. They could frame and compose a portrait
that really saw the person for who they were. When they shared
their work, some cried because they felt so seen and heard.

It is a challenge to get people to set aside enough time to truly
encounter another person. When we always need to keep going,
to speed up or die, setting aside a few days is a big sacrifice. To
a person, those who did take the time thought it was worth it.
But they still did not know how to convince someone else of its
worth. They could point to their portrait or their poem, but it
was not about producing something. A class could teach them

those skills. In our debriefs we gently told them that maybe the value of the experience was found in the encounter. This resonated with them. They wanted more but were unsure how to go about it.

After PEEL, congregations and ministries did their own experiment. They have tried to hear each other by creating ways and means for confession to happen, as described in chapter 3. When we watched the Ansari video together, it resonated with their experience of really hearing another. How can we create something that helps others do that? They have tried to see others in all of their complexity. Whom do we look past, even those we "see" all the time, so that the image of God gets obscured? All of this has led to two different outcomes. First, they want to encounter God. In people, they see glimpses of God and hear whispers of the Spirit. Second, they want to serve others and, in turn, be served. As they saw and heard each other in PEEL, they started to delight in each other. That delight leads to serving one another.

### The Second Move: Encounter God

Encountering another person has great value in and of itself. If your church could create places where people can be seen and heard, that would be a win for the kingdom. The quality of our relationships as we wait on God matters, and we can and should spend time tending to them. But that is only one part of the waiting that God calls us to. In the end, what we know and hope for is that we will encounter God.

Theologian Karl Barth has a famous passage (well, let's be real, theologians are hardly "famous," but it is well known within some small circles of Christians) where he says that we can encounter God in many different places because it is God who does the revealing.[4] We can encounter God in a blossoming shrub, a Mozart concerto, or a dead dog because God can use anything that God wants to reveal God's self. Many stop there and limit themselves to blossoming shrubs and dazzling sunsets, hoping that in the awe and beauty of the world, they will see God. (Strangely, few do that with dead dogs.) But Barth says that while God *can* use sunsets, concertos, or dead dogs, God *does* use certain things. We would do well to attend to those places and times that God has set out as moments of encounter. Barth's advice is to not chase sunsets, concertos, or dead dogs, because they are not a sure thing. Instead, look to preaching, prayer, and mission as places we might encounter God.

In the chapters that follow you will see examples of real-life churches meeting God in each of these places. At Queenston United Church it was preaching, and at Peace Lutheran it was prayer. Sometimes they encounter God in more than one practice. Before we highlight and point to those places where the church meets God, we want to connect how an encounter with another person prepares us to encounter God.

## Hearing God

When we hear another person, we have a chance to encounter. So where do we hear God? In the reading of God's written word, the Bible. The Bible witnesses to God's relationship with God's people and the world over a long period of time. The Old Testament continually reminds us to remember, to tell the stories again and again, to know that the God who saved in the past will save again. Deuteronomy 6 goes so far as to say:

> Keep these words that I am commanding you today in your heart. Recite them to your children and talk about them when

you are at home and when you are away, when you lie down and when you rise. Bind them as a sign on your hand, fix them as an emblem on your forehead, and write them on the doorposts of your house and on your gates. (Deut. 6:6–9)

God's people are a storied people, and they need continual reminding.

This isn't just limited to the Old Testament. Remember the disciples on the road to Emmaus in Luke? When Jesus breaks the bread and prays, they see him for who he really is. Before that, Luke 24:27 tells us that "beginning with Moses and all the prophets, he interpreted to them the things about himself in all the scriptures." Before prayer, Jesus did Bible study with them. Besides the fact that all of Acts recalls stories from the Old Testament, it is clear that the Bible plays a key role in the life of the community. As it is with all leaders in the church, at some point people were not happy with the apostles (see Acts 6:1–7). "They spend too much time in Bible study! Where does that get us? We need to be out there feeding the hungry." The apostles recognize the problem as a choice between two good things, the Bible and mission. They don't stop reading and preaching the Bible. They recruit more leaders so that both can happen.

Throughout Christian history, almost every revival we know of starts with a renewed reading of the Bible. Christians gather around the word and wait for God to speak. It might seem obvious but perhaps not. Waiting means that God can surprise us, shake us up, move us. Waiting makes God the star of the show. Missional theologian Darrell Guder proposes five questions that ensure God remains the main character of the biblical story:

1. What is God's good news in this text? (the gospel question)

2. What conversion does God call for in this text? (the change question)

3. What does God reveal about us and the world in this text? (the context question)

4. What does this text reveal about God's future? (the eschatological question)

5. Where does God send us through this text? (the mission question)

Guder has used variations of these for a number of years, but they are always trying to point to the same thing: God speaks to us through the Bible. Once we hear, we can proclaim the gospel, change our behavior, better understand the world, hope for the future, and go out into the world. But before we hear, we must wait attentively.

## Seeing God

The church throughout the centuries has said that the place where we see God is in the sacraments. This is not the *only* place, but it is definitely a premier place. If we know that God shows up there, shouldn't we pay attention to that? It makes little difference to us whether you are a smells-and-bells Roman Catholic or a plain and staid Baptist. The important affirmations are that God reveals God's self in visible signs, that these signs draw our attention to God's action in the world, and that we do these things together. To be more precise, we are less focused on sacraments (seven vs. two vs. three, consubstantiation vs. transubstantiation, etc.) and more focused on the sacramental.

For instance, we know some Mennonites who practice foot washing. For them, it is sacramental even if it is not a sacrament.

Jesus told his disciples to do it, the water is a physical sign (to say nothing of the stinky feet), and it is a moment that must include more than one person. In doing it, they remind themselves of Maundy Thursday, when Jesus took the form of a servant, calling the apostles friends and giving them a new commandment. There is a story wrapped up in that moment, one that becomes beautiful and profound and formative when it is repeated in the act. Theological debates do not change the fact that the story shapes us in deep ways.

Others we know consider anointing the sick with oil to be sacramental. While Jesus did not command it, he did do a lot of healing. The oil is a sign, and we do it on behalf of another. Besides the command given in the book of James, the anointing of the sick reminds us of all the other anointings in the Bible, from the anointing of kings to the women going to the empty tomb. We see God at work in the past as we do God's work in the moment.

Each of these actions takes place in the context of prayer. There is no magic at work here. This is not Harry Potter, where if we say the right words and wave our wand just right, God will apparate before us. Prayer in this sacramental way is to wait for God to act. We open our eyes to God's action in the world by doing something sacramental. We have the promise from God that, in some way that we do not totally understand, God will be present there.

### Serving God

When we believe that God acts only in the church, we think our mission is to bring to others something that only we have. As if God were a product, a possession, something we can know and the world can't. The story of the red paint and Grace

Presbyterian (from chap. 3) demonstrates how the world can bring a prophetic word to the church and how the church can wait to hear that word even as it acts in ways that witness to the gospel. But the story of Grace Presbyterian also shows that it is hard to see and hear God in the world without first preparing for that.

A watchword often arrives within the church but in relation to the world. Consider Martin Luther King Jr. again. His struggle for civil rights was obviously in the world. The watchword, "Out of no way, God makes a way," spoke to the entire civil rights movement. At the same time, it came to King when he was at his kitchen table, attending to Scripture in prayer, concerned as a father and a husband. His watchword was for him and the struggles that he faced. There are no hard-and-fast rules to God revealing a watchword, but look for it at the margins of your life together, where the church and the world meet.

# 7

# Out of the Family Basement

As Howard would tell it, all good things in his life had come
through the United Church of Christ. He met his wife at a small
prairie church, received his calling at a small suburban congregation, and was now baptizing his children in a small semi-
rural church. The larger denominational structure had value
for Howard, especially as it connected him to other Christians
around the country and the world and supported the life and
work of congregations, but it was in the small sanctuaries that
he found God. Whether the carpet was blue or red, the pews
padded or bare, the flowers real or fake, Howard felt at home
in these small, traditional sanctuaries. He had a place for the
contemporary, but he felt that the traditional got a bad name.
As he stood in front of his small flock in his small sanctuary,
he had a large sense that God was present.

Howard did value the new and contemporary, though, when
it came to how small congregations did food, which was anything but new and contemporary. Things, he felt, could afford

to change when it came to congregational dinners. Anyone familiar with church potlucks of yesteryear may remember Fiesta Carrot Pineapple Jell-O salad, which despite the rebranding (adding Fiesta is a nice touch) is still not served as a dessert at most restaurants. There's a reason for that, Howard would note. Restaurants only serve food that they can sell. Fiesta Carrot Pineapple Jell-O salad must be given away. And while there is nothing inherently wrong with free, bizarre dessert concoctions, there is nothing especially right about them either. Some of the small churches that Howard knew compounded this menu faux pas with something more objectively wrong: cramped quarters. A cramped basement filled with stacked tables, a cramped kitchen filled to the brim with castoffs, and cramped stairs filled with people coming up and down. The facilities were unsuited to the purpose. They were neither comfortable nor efficient nor accessible. For Howard, the way that the small church approached food needed some new thinking.

This was not Howard's first rodeo at a small church. He knew that small churches fall prey to two traps that reinforce each other. First, small churches see themselves as a family. While this is theologically sound—after all, Jesus calls us brothers and sisters—it is sociologically complicated. At times it is *too* true. Small churches tend to have members who are less mobile (not moving from place to place), and thus the membership roll has a high degree of stability. It is not uncommon for extended families rooted in a place to attend the same church. One or two families can dominate the membership, and because they stick around for a long time, they also make the decisions. Pastors come and go, but patriarchs and matriarchs stay. Just as you wouldn't invite yourself to someone's house for Thanksgiving, if a church has a few dominant families, you might not feel particularly invited to "their" house. The people who are there, the "family," like how things have been, they find comfort in it, they have some ownership over the goings-on. Newcomers? Less so.

This leads into the second trap: the endowment effect. Economists and behavioral psychologists note that we tend to overestimate the value of the things we own. Because we like something and have invested in it, we assume that others like it and are therefore willing to invest the same amount. Any real estate agent can confirm the existence of the endowment effect. We consistently look past the oddities in our home because it is *our* home. What we count as charm or character others might look at as weird or problematic. We like a certain color of paint or style of wallpaper, only to discover that others are wondering how we ever thought that was a good idea. Then comes a rude awakening on the day we need to sell our house: no one else wants to pay a premium for that odd feature. "What do you mean we have to paint over that wall!? It's beautiful! Everyone loves *chartreuse*!" We confuse our personal taste and choice, the things that comfort us and that we have invested in, with what most other people would find comforting and want to invest in.

A small church that thinks of itself as a family also tends toward the endowment effect. The dank basement had been dug out by a previous generation of members and thus has value. Work parties, capital campaigns, and real blood, sweat, and tears shed by their family went into the building of that basement. Not to mention the financial sacrifice that generations have made. The building is better than before, a fact that long-standing members know and remember and value. But newcomers don't remember; they don't value the basement or endow it with meaning. What they see is a dank basement. Likewise, the cramped stairs. No one at the small church has a wheelchair, so they can't understand why they might need to become more accessible. Why would I make my house accessible if I like it the way it is? Why do we need an elevator if none of us are in a wheelchair? But any newcomer sees immediately that those with mobility challenges will struggle to participate fully in the life of the congregation. Is coming again worth it for the newcomer? Not likely. They could go to another church, but they will likely just not go to church at all.

These considerations just made basic business sense for Howard. He knew that there was a push toward being entrepreneurial in his denomination. The mindset of an entrepreneur seemed to overlap with the missional theology he had studied at seminary. An entrepreneur looks at the needs and wants of potential customers; a church should look at the needs and wants of those in their catchment area. Entrepreneurs and churches could not afford to act like families, overvaluing stability and their own way of doing things. Howard supported the efforts to make the church more focused on the needs of others rather than the needs of those who already attended. In truth, Howard was at Queenston UCC to do this very task.

Like many small churches, Queenston UCC struggled. Even small changes in local demographics have a large effect on a small congregation. For the first time in three generations, the two main families of Queenston UCC were not replacing themselves. One family, the Thurstons, had cut back on their farming, and so most of their children had moved away to find work elsewhere. The other, the Winds, had children and grandchildren who were relatively local but never seemed to show up to church. One had married a devout Roman Catholic, another was going to a large Baptist congregation in the adjoining county, and the other two seemed disinterested in regularly attending Queenston UCC. There was a Thurston patriarch and a Wind matriarch attending, but their families were not. With the general demographic trends leading to decline across mainline denominations, Queenston UCC was one or two deaths away from closing.

Howard was too good a minister for Queenston UCC to even consider recruiting as their pastor, except that he was attending a nearby seminary and had to be in the area. His wife also had a good job at a local school. Howard would be sticking around for two to five years. He couldn't imagine not preaching every Sunday. He was a preacher, after all, and what is a preacher without a pulpit? All the other nearby UCC churches had incumbents, so Queenston lucked into getting a dynamic, young minister. They were under no illusions, however. They knew that Howard was at best a caretaker minister but more likely an undertaker; he would look after them and their pastoral needs till the church died. Most of the leaders were past the stage of believing that Queenston UCC could become a vibrant community church again. But they didn't want to just quietly fade away either. Howard offered them a dynamic preacher but for a limited time. It was a match made in heaven.

But Howard was not content being either a caretaker or an undertaker. He was a pastor. His call did not come from people, as much as he loved small UCC churches. His call came from God. Howard never had a Damascus road experience, but he did have a clear and driving sense of mission, which he credited to God. As a young man, trying to figure out what he wanted to do with his life, Howard had come upon John 21:15–17, where Jesus commands Peter to first "feed my lambs" and then "tend my sheep" and finally "feed my sheep." There wasn't a particular moment, no sermon or lesson, that stuck out. But time and again he came back to John 21, and it struck something deep within Howard. As a young man he had witnessed seeing someone get bullied because of the way that they looked. It struck him with lightning clarity that this was the lamb whom Jesus had gone hunting for, the one whom he entreated Peter to tend, the one who needed feeding. The powerful would prey upon the sheep, but Jesus had instructed his disciples to look after them. Not everyone needed to become a pastor, but from Howard's perspective everyone needed to be pastoral. Not all are called to shepherd a congregation, but the church as a whole is called to look after the sheep, to tend them, to feed them.

As Howard grew up, first taking a career path in communications, John 21 kept coming back to him—*feed my sheep*. He was good at his job in communications, but he sensed that he needed to use those skills for a different purpose. Instead of selling products, Howard felt that he should communicate the love and grace and acceptance of God found in Jesus Christ. The leadership of his UCC congregation started to rely on him more and more in the pulpit, even as he made them a bit uncomfortable. They loved when he would fill in for the regular preacher, his sermons always hitting home but always challenging them in his dogged insistence that the church could do better to go and find the lost sheep, to protect the most vulnerable, to offer something of substance to those outside their tiny congregation. Long before the days when being a "social justice warrior" was considered an insult, Howard coupled strong biblical preaching with a deep commitment to sticking up for the underdog.

This commitment to helping the most vulnerable caused Howard's discomfort with the way Queenston UCC did food. It had a few annual events centered on food, even a turkey dinner around Thanksgiving, and these were technically open to the community, but few except church members came. What would it take to break out of the church basement, out of the endowment effect and holding a family dinner, and instead truly reach out to the lost sheep in their community? Howard brought his own personal watchword—feed my sheep—to Queenston, and it started to work itself out in powerful ways.

## Feed My Sheep

When Howard arrived as the new minister, there were about fifteen people actively involved in the congregation. These low numbers challenged the congregation's financial viability. It also put pressure on Howard. As a graduate student, father of two young children, and husband to a wife with a demanding job, time was tight. But Howard could not imagine life without Sunday morning in the pulpit. For him, he went to school so that what he learned would support the life of the church. But if he wasn't in the congregation week in and week out, it was hard to bridge the divide between school and church. Though few in number, the remaining members could be described as resilient, gritty, and tough. They weren't going down without a bit of energy. Add to this the fact that Howard firmly believed that the word of God could resurrect the dead. More revival preacher than undertaker, he embodied the best passion of an old-school circuit rider with the theology that inspired Martin Luther King Jr. He didn't feed people hellfire and brimstone. He fed them words of life. Week in and week out, he preached the Bible, not shying away from hard questions but always tending to the flock before him.

With Howard's arrival came some other people who he had met. They were newcomers to the area. Some came from the school where his wife taught. Others came from the university. Roughly ten in number, they came for different reasons but all were somehow spiritual refugees. Some wanted to escape the pressure of worshiping with people they worked with at the university. Others felt that other churches were too big. Still others resonated with Howard's preaching. They all felt there was life at Queenston UCC. Worship became a mixture of longtime members, such as the Thurstons and Winds, whose place in the church went back three generations, and newcomers, mostly younger and from other parts of the country. Each week, they gathered in the small sanctuary and came to the table together. Howard initiated weekly communion, which was met with some resistance at first. Newcomers didn't know any different. Long-timers put up with it because they liked Howard and he was still in the honeymoon phase with them.

It helped that Howard continued the tradition of everyone standing at the end of the service, gathering in a large circle around the sanctuary, holding hands, and singing. All church growth literature would say this is a bad idea. Did we mention the holding hands part? Forcing people to touch each other? Sing? Insane. This is something a family might do. But newcomers? Not so much. Eventually Howard transitioned out of the hand-holding part, but the rest stayed. It was part of Queenston UCC's charm. As corny and as ill-advised as that circle might have been, it started and ended at the table. Quite literally, the circle started with Howard beside the communion table and, as the congregation slowly grew, stretched along the side, across the back, and down the other aisle till it met again at the communion table. At this table they fed on God's grace.

Slowly, through repetition and discussion, prayer and study, Queenston UCC became aware of Howard's personal watchword—feed my sheep. Howard fed the sheep in his preaching. The wonderful and eclectic and strange community gathered to be fed at the table. But for Howard there was one more step. The preaching was good, the circle with the sacraments in the middle was good, but there was no reaching out to the lost sheep. It took a another local church to connect this new and tender watchword—feed my sheep—with an outreach ministry suitable to what God was doing.

This nondenominational church not too far from Queenston UCC had been holding fundraising dinners to support the construction of a new church building. While they were in the process of construction, they were homeless. The new building was not ready, nor did they own the old building. Renting a small worship space in a strip mall meant that they no longer had a kitchen or the resources to continue their fundraising dinners. With a bit of entrepreneurial gumption, this church thought outside their building. What did they have? A parking lot: at the rented strip mall and later at their new building. How could they make money with that in a town that didn't have a great need for paid parking? The idea they fell on came to them by watching a Roman Catholic service club. The Knights of Columbus owned a BBQ trailer that they hauled around to local events such as the fall fair. They only sold one thing, beef on a bun, but it seemed to make a profit. This nondenominational church also noted that there were many food-truck festivals that happened throughout the community. Why not invite food trucks, including the Knights of Columbus, to have a Friday night Food Truck Fest?

The event started out a bit rocky, but after some trial and error, they figured out the right combination of timing and trucks to make it a win for everyone. The food trucks made a profit, and the church got a cut of those profits for hosting and advertising. It didn't raise a lot of money, but it was better than nothing. One Friday night during report-card season, while his wife was working late, Howard was buying dinner for his kids at the food trucks. He noticed several other solo parents as well as a group of seniors chatting away. Some skater kids off in the corner of the parking lot alternated between eating and doing tricks on the concrete divider. These people either lacked families to eat with, even temporarily, or didn't want to eat with their given family. They were choosing to be together in a parking lot with a bunch of food trucks. It was then that Howard realized that Queenston UCC could "feed my sheep" by getting a food truck. There was a venue (the nondenominational church would continue to host for the foreseeable future) and precedent (the Roman Catholics did it).

The time between the birth of this idea and its actuality was not neat or tidy, but the messiness should not obscure the fact that Queenston UCC took their watchword so seriously that they went out and bought a food truck to do outreach ministry. "Feed my sheep" shaped their imagination in such a way that they could see a direct path from getting spiritually fed on Sunday morning through the table where the community gathered to feast on Christ's presence to reaching out to the community with food. Despite all the hard work and stress and discussions and worries, it was awesome. Eventually.

## From Howard to Trevor

For Queenston UCC, as with many small churches, their discovery of a watchword came from their pastor. When we focus on survival or on how things were done in the past, we can't see what God is doing in our midst. It takes an outsider to bring something fresh. What started from a dark moment in Howard's life, witnessing a graphic scene of bullying, crystallized into something that guided everything he did. "Feed my sheep" became a word not just to an individual but to a whole group. God's word to Howard had meaning beyond what he could imagine even while he pastored these people. When he proposed to his small group of church leaders that they buy a food truck, they were skeptical. But without too much cajoling and far more witnessing, Howard showed them how it fit with who they were becoming. On a practical level, it made sense, oddly enough. They struggled with their events around food. By moving their kitchen outside, they would get out of the basement. They also had vague ideas about using it for providing disaster relief (hurricane recovery, etc.) and as a potential outreach to local communities. What Howard saw more clearly than the others was that having a food truck could lead to a deep-seated heart change. Instead of just looking inward, they might look outward and find God already there. Feeding my sheep could revitalize their worship and their witness to God's grace.

These potential benefits came against a backdrop of a much less awesome reality familiar to small church leaders everywhere. The bills still needed paying. The denomination wanted the congregation to fund itself. It was willing to provide grants, but those grants would run out at some point. And grants require grant writing. Grant writing requires long hours of selling yourself in just the way the granting organization wants. Long hours require much labor. And much labor, in a small church, usually falls on the pastor. This is the exhausting cycle we described in some detail in the first chapters. While the watchword was bringing vibrant life to the congregation, in the background, the logic of decline was working against it.

Howard actually left the church before the dream of the food truck came to be. Everyone, including Howard, was sad for him to leave, but the time had come. His studies were done, and there was a larger church calling him. While the leaders of Queenston UCC wished he could have stayed, they were realistic about his commitment. During Howard's tenure, attendance had doubled. If a larger church had gone from 500 to 1,000 in the time that Queenston UCC had gone from 15 to 30, whole books would have been written about them. Howard didn't dwell on that fact, instead focusing on the sense of God's presence in worship, but the leaders certainly did. Nothing but gratitude came at his going-away dinner (ironically held in the church basement, to Howard's chagrin).

With Howard's departure to another church, Trevor became the pastor. Trevor was a go-get-'em kind of guy. He never saw an idea he didn't like, spinning them off at a dizzying rate. People loved his can-do attitude and winsome charisma. Trevor's natural habitat was not the pulpit but the meeting room. Worship remained traditional but now a bit more folksy, almost informal. With Trevor in place and hard at work, the grants and funding required to buy a food truck came to be. There were lay leaders involved in the efforts, but Trevor did a lot of the legwork, using his connections in the denominational office and beyond. Like Howard before him, he had a lot to juggle. But, also like Howard, he jumped in with both feet.

One of Trevor's passions was youth ministry. He really wanted to reach the student community. Year by year, more and more young people made their way out to Queenston UCC. Rough math suggests that from Howard's first days to Trevor's last days, attendance grew roughly 800 percent. Such growth is exceptional, but it doesn't solve the problem of decline. Young people have energy and can sniff out the presence of God, but they don't have the dollars to make a church run. Their presence affirms the church in its watchword. More sheep get fed. But it also drives the crisis of decline to new depths. More people require more money, and if those people don't bring it, the church must find it somewhere. What many small churches think is the solution—more young people!—actually hastens the dynamics leading to decline.

Importantly, the students were coming but not because they encountered the church through the food truck. As a tool for evangelism, the truck had limited success. The truck made its rounds to the nondenominational church's parking lot and back, providing an outdoor kitchen, but it was never really used for disaster relief or outreach. Yet there was an energy, a vibrancy, at Queenston UCC that often gets lost at other churches, if it ever appears. The new people, along with the longtime members, felt fed, but the food truck had become less connected to the watchword than the other two dimensions of preaching and community. The disconnection was more than just a vague feeling: for tax and business reasons, Trevor decided it best that the food truck continue as a separate 501(c)(3) organization. The church hired one of its own, a former fast-food restaurant manager, to be the director of the food truck. The energy at Queenston UCC hid the fact that the food truck wasn't doing all it had set out to do. It also hid the fact that there had been a direct challenge to their watchword. A subtle but profound change had happened. The watchword—feed my sheep—remained, but it got competition.

### You Are Loved and You Are Enough

Pretty early in his ministry, Trevor introduced a phrase into his welcome-to-worship message. Every Sunday, after announcements, he ended his welcome with, "You are loved and you are enough." If he hadn't said it every Sunday, it might have been thought of as a throwaway comment. But he repeated it. People expected it. Like the circle at the end of the service, this phrase became part of Queenston UCC. New members often indicated that the moment they heard Trevor say that phrase, they knew Queenston UCC was for them. It spoke to people.

Well, it spoke to *most* people. Some within leadership had questions. The first part, "you are loved," was something everyone could get behind, although some wanted clarifications. Who is doing the loving? God? Queenston UCC? Trevor? Some other anonymous person? And doesn't saying "you are loved" put too much emphasis on the individual? The argument could go that this phrase is saying that God loves the world and we as individuals are included in that love. The counter-argument is that love always has an object. We cannot love in abstract, so what do we really mean by "the world"? God must love a person, an individual, in order to love the world. These might seem like small things—who is doing the loving isn't clear, and it is aimed at an individual—but if a watchword is supposed to capture God's activity, a story, and if it is to shape us into a faithful people, even small nuances can have large consequences. By obscuring the subject and using "you," are we making the gospel more about the individual and their feelings than about God and God's love for the entire world? What does a church focused on the individual rather than the community look like?

But the really tough questions concerned the second part of the phrase, "and you are enough." A key part of the gospel message seems to be the exact opposite of the plain meaning of this phrase. If we were enough, we would not need God, because then we could just save ourselves. Our inadequacy makes salvation into such a gracious gift from God. Paired with the first part, it is possible to understand this phrase as "God loves you just the way you are." In some sense, this is true. As Paul puts it, while we were yet sinners, God came to save us (Rom. 5:8). God loved us even when we were sinners. For this to square with all that we know of God, though, we also need to add something like, "God loved you so much that God wouldn't let you stay the way you were." We were lost, and God loved us so much when we were lost that he sent Jesus to find us. God saves us. Being saved, we live into a fuller life of grace. Theologians use the term "sanctification" to describe how the Holy Spirit makes us holier and holier. If we are enough, do we need saving? Do we need to change?

This phrase lands differently for different people. Some of the newcomers heard a message of affirmation. In their previous church experiences, they may have heard the opposite of "you are enough." "You must earn God's love because you are a worm" is the implicit message of moralism pretending to be the gospel. Is it any wonder that those who felt burned by such moralism in the church would welcome this new phrase? The good news always answers some bad news. If you are hungry, good news is food. If you are lost, good news is a way. If you feel rejected, good news sounds like acceptance.

We suspect that Trevor used this phrase because it was both spiritual and effective. Though not straight from the Bible, it sounds Christian at first read. There is a certain ambiguity that allows the listener to provide their own meaning. The watchword "feed my sheep" also had ambiguity, but it seemed more like a productive mystery. For instance, in this watchword, we are able to see ourselves as both sheep (we need feeding) and shepherds (we need to go and feed). "Feed my sheep" has a direct biblical context that helps to guide and inform how it plays out in the life of God's people. It balances comfort, coming to God in need of shepherding, and challenge, going into God's world to look after God's people. It can fuel our practical imagination. Much less so with "You are loved and you are enough."

Yet, with the huge jump in attendance, the phrase was obviously effective at communicating that Queenston UCC was a place for people to come and belong. If it works, keep doing it! That is a mantra thoroughly at home within the accelerated secular age. As we've shown, working faster and longer is never enough. The leaders of Queenston UCC found this to be true. No matter how much people gave, no matter how many grants Trevor secured, no matter how much they did, enough was always just a step ahead. "You are loved and you are enough" became an indictment because they didn't feel they were enough. Quite the opposite. In the end, Trevor was exhausted, as were the key leaders, both new and old. After three years of intense growth and energy and ministry, Trevor called it quits. Like Howard before him, a larger church (with more resources and more people than Trevor could resist) called him.

## Watchwords Need Champions

Both large churches and small churches will have watchwords that come and go. As time goes by, a watchword will become less vital until the day that another watchword arrives. In those transitions, the longevity of the senior pastor and the size of the church can play a significant role. At Queenston UCC, the transition from one watchword to another proved tumultuous. If there had been a longtime pastor who could have guided that transition, the process might have been smoother. A long-tenured pastor might have known better what to listen for, where to look, and how to help others do so as well. By moving from Howard to Trevor in about seven years, Queenston UCC did not have a pastor who could give that direction. A kind of competition arose between the old and the new watchword because there was no one to guide the process.

The reality is that in small churches, pastors may come and pastors may go, but the founding families stay. With Queenston UCC, this shuffling of pastors was due to how their denomination hired ministers. In this situation, the founding families are like teachers, and the pastors like students. Teachers know that students come and go, but the teachers remain. Don't like these students? Don't worry, you just need to hang on for a while till you get rid of them.

Watchwords come from an experience of God. Through preaching and worship, Howard passed on his watchword to the little group made up mostly of founding families. As more people came, as time passed, and as Howard departed, fewer people at the church could draw on a direct relationship with Howard, nor had they experienced the vitality of living out the watchword. They couldn't remember because they weren't there. Even for those who were there, the memory had faded. Believe us, as middle-aged guys, when we say that encounters with God from thirty years ago are not as fresh as they once were. A regular practice of testimony can keep some of these encounters new, but we don't often have a context in which people can tell those stories. At Queenston UCC this memory atrophy sped up because of changing pastors and the nature of the newcomers. What might have taken a decade at a church with a long-tenured pastor (such as Peace Lutheran, which we'll hear about in the next chapter) happened in four years at Queenston UCC.

Every watchword starts with a champion. In this case, Howard. But every watchword also needs a champion who is not the pastor. It was Howard's responsibility to feed the sheep. The pastor preaches, tends the table, and sends people out into the world. To get the pastor caught up in the day-to-day workings of a food truck, which is what happened with Trevor, is to confuse their role. For a small church, the pastor must equip those who will be there once the pastor leaves to hear the watchword and then amplify it in their life together. If the pastor is the only one who has the watchword, it will disappear with them, even if God is not yet done with it.

## Feeding My Sheep in a Different Way

Shortly after Trevor's departure, Queenston UCC sold their food truck. It had become a burden both financially and practically. It needed costly repairs that the church couldn't pay for. They were using it less frequently, as the food-truck festival shifted with the changing needs of the nondenominational church. If the leaders were being honest, it required a lot of work for something that didn't directly contribute to their bottom line. What had once flowed as a natural outworking from their watchword was now a drag on their effective innovation. Another church several counties over had taken notice of the truck sitting in the parking lot. They asked about using it for an outreach to those living on the streets in their community. Local laws had changed such that they couldn't easily coordinate the food distribution. With a food truck, though, they could keep feeding the hungry and stay within the law. After some very amicable negotiations, the food truck was sold.

The real crisis that Queenston UCC faced was not one of decline. The real crisis, as always, is how to encounter the God who is God. Leaders of small churches might read this and ask themselves, What is the moral of this story? There might be something we take away, but the moral of the story is not that this is a narrative of decline to be avoided. Morality tales are the stories we tell others to warn them away from our mistakes. When we say, for example, "Those who cannot remember the past are condemned to repeat it," we start a morality tale. History, if we study it, reveals why and how certain things happened. The implication is that, if we don't do those things, we can have a different, more successful outcome. "If only we had done . . ." ends most morality tales. In the morality tale, to remember history is to remember the mistakes we made as we moved toward success.

Watchwords remember an encounter. They point to a time and place where God showed God. The story of Queenston UCC could be the story of a church near death that becomes successful (as measured by the secular age). An 800 percent attendance increase! Or it could be the story of God's people waiting till God showed up. We opt for the second approach. It is possible that small church leaders could walk away from the example of Queenston UCC thinking, *Well, we shouldn't do that.* We'd be sad if that happened. Queenston UCC experienced a profound moment of God acting in the life of God's people. We should not lose sight of that fact. The purchase of the food truck was the culmination of a watchword that had started when Howard in his youth witnessed someone being bullied. In this telling, the sale of the food truck fit well with the watchword "Feed my sheep." In the days before the food truck was sold, it wasn't feeding sheep. It was sitting in a parking lot. Selling it released God's presence into the world. Admittedly, it did so in ways that Queenston UCC did not imagine, but it was wonderful and beautiful that hungry people got fed.

It was an audacious move to buy a food truck. It took a chutzpah that can only come from a place of radical faith. Truth be told, we have a deep admiration (even love) for each character in this story. They jumped into an unknown future equipped with only hope in a watchword that God had given them—feed my sheep. If only all of us were so faithful.

Not every small church should buy a food truck. To conclude that is to see this story as some version of a morality tale. The morality tale leads to a list of don'ts: don't do this, don't make this mistake. Or it could become a to-do list. Do this and you will succeed. If you walk away thinking that buying a food truck or any other social innovation is the silver bullet to solving the crisis of decline, you missed the point.

If there were anything approximating a lesson, it would be to note the fragility of a watchword. It comes in a moment of death (in this case, the extreme bullying witnessed by Howard and the near death of the congregation), and it carries us into life. But we often forget that. Other concerns, such as the crisis of decline, can distract us from our first love. We might continue to hold a form of that watchword. It stays on our website, but it becomes an empty shell. The joy and excitement we found in that God encounter fades. God is not done in the story of Queenston UCC or their food truck or your church. Remember your God and let that encounter shape your life together.

# 8

# Nothing Can Separate You

They were two very odd birds. But why wouldn't they be? You have to be odd to love being a seventh-grade Sunday school teacher. Twenty-two years ago—just after coming to the church—pastor Mike Woods discovered the importance of a watchword. He didn't call it a watchword then—he wouldn't even call it that now—but for the last two decades, a watchword has been central to his ministry. This watchword has revitalized his congregation. The centrality of the watchword goes back to those odd birds, Margie and Gene Jurgenson, and their strange way of teaching Sunday school.

Pastor Mike came to Prince of Peace Lutheran Church in 1999. The church has hovered around three hundred people in worship for the last few decades. Mike came to the suburban Prince of Peace from the rural prairies of his first call in North Dakota, ready to take on the world. Coming with all the "correct" Lutheran theological answers, Mike was ready to preach hard and fast the gospel of Jesus Christ. Mike was sure (and had been assured by his professors) that the correct form of preaching, mixed with bold leadership—a bravado echoing back to Martin Luther himself—would transform any congregation. And Mike figured that Prince of Peace needed transformation. It needed a boost in relevance and membership. It was a solid church, being led with faithfulness by senior pastor Jim Arends. Mike would be the associate, figuring his job was to throw some gas on what Jim was already doing. Everyone assumed that with these two dynamos, the exponential energy they'd produce would change the church, would beat back any specters of decline. Just think of the ideas this tag team of pastors could craft from their own creativity. In La Crescent, Minnesota, a bedroom community, in the late 1990s, there were not a lot of frontal signs of decline. But the decline that was happening in Milwaukee and Chicago was reaching them steadily, though slightly. Mike's hiring was intended to fortify against those threats of deterioration.

Mike began by successfully organizing the programs, wielding his creativity. Things seemed to move forward. He was tightening down each part of the congregation's educational ministry, helping teachers and mentors run their classrooms and programs with excellence. And yet something felt ever so slightly amiss, like an American visiting Canada (or, to be fair to our Canadian friends, a Canadian visiting America). At first glance everything seemed to be in the right place: Sunday school was running like it was supposed to be. Yet, after a second look, things appeared just a degree or two off; something unusual was happening in one of those classrooms. Mike couldn't make sense of what felt off. He also couldn't make sense of the Jurgensons. All the other teachers and leaders seemed to follow Mike's expertise perfectly, taking his direction, soaking up his leadership like a sponge. That's how Mike was told in seminary it would go. It was all trickling down, just as they taught him. Mike formed the leaders, giving them the formula for an excellent class with good theology, and they, in turn, implemented it. All of them but those pesky Jurgensons. They were off script. And they seemed to have little interest in learning their lines.

Mike became privy to how off script they were when he kept finding them and their group of seventh graders in the oddest places. He often found them under the table in their classroom, all pulled together, whispering and giggling. Other times, Mike found them in the boiler room or some other strange place in the church building. This was not how Mike imagined a successful Sunday school class. But Mike couldn't deny the passion of the Jurgensons. He couldn't quite crack the code on why this corny couple, in the last third of their lives, was so engaging to seventh graders. But they'd been at this a lot longer than Mike.

Mike kept hearing stories of how the Jurgensons called each kid in their class on their birthday and sang to them. People reported to Mike that they still got a birthday call from them even after being out of seventh grade for ten years. Learning this, Mike decided it wasn't wise to force the Jurgensons to conform to his ways. So, he watched. He waited.

In that watching-turned-into-waiting, he couldn't deny the resonance of the group. The seventh graders hung on every word, praying together and asking big questions. They were all engaged and searching with the Jurgensons for the God who is God. Mike couldn't deny this. His own mystical propensities wouldn't allow him to deny it. He felt drawn to it; he wished he were in their class. He even wished on his birthday that he'd get a call. Mike started deeply admiring the Jurgensons. He wasn't sure why they were such good Sunday school teachers, but he was certain that they were. This led Mike to give up his assumptions of program conformity, to let go of needing to be the expert, and to just be the pastor. He knew he had something to learn from the Jurgensons.

One day Mike asked them directly, "How did the two of you become such great Sunday school teachers?" In what seemed like classic Upper Midwest self-deprecation, Gene Jurgenson responded, "Oh, we're not good Sunday school teachers at all." Mike tilted his head and widened his eyes to communicate that he didn't believe it. "It's true," Gene insisted, "we really only have one message, and it's always, every single time, that same message. We don't know what else to say or do. Even when you give us all sorts of those lessons and help, we just keep coming back to the same one message. We honestly don't know what else to teach."

Deeply intrigued, Mike asked, "What's the one message?"

Somehow possessing both confidence and unassuredness, Gene Jurgenson said, "We just keep saying, 'Nothing can separate us from God's love.' We just keep teaching that. We tried to teach other things, but we just keep coming back to those words every time. That's all we do." With a cringe Margie Jurgenson said, "I guess we only have that one lesson." A silence came between Mike and the Jurgensons. Misreading the silence's poignant nature, Gene responded, "Sorry."

But there was no reason to apologize. The Jurgensons weren't doing something wrong. They had just pushed Mike into an extra dimension of leadership, and the congregation into a new way of being. Mike communicated to them as much. He told them not to stop, that they weren't doing anything wrong, and that the rest of the congregation could learn from it. When Mike told pastor Jim what the Jurgensons had told him, Jim confirmed that somehow this was a word for the whole church. It soon became their watchword.

Margie Jurgenson had already stitched the watchword on a banner. Months earlier, Mike had thought the banner a little trite and old-fashioned. Now it was soaked with meaning. Mike and Jim moved the banner to the center of the sanctuary. They began referring to the watchword in their sermons, meetings, and other teaching times. If you look back at their staff reports and minutes, this watchword pops up in 2004, framing their description of the church's ministries, serving as a lens of discernment, sinking into the congregation's identity.

At every chance, Mike and Jim kept saying to the church to remember, "Nothing can separate us from God's love. This is a God who stands with and for us, on our side." It was forming the congregation. They were waiting with this word, being together around this word. Their imagination had been formed to look for God through the lens of this word. It was so much more than a slogan, so much more than all the other generic phrases. Both Mike and Jim had struggled with not having a mission statement. They had inherited a long, essay-length treatise of purpose from the previous pastor. But it didn't ring true. And yet they felt the pressure to come up with their own mission statement. Nothing clicked. Other churches were drawing from national church revitalization programs to find direction. Mike and Jim knew a handful of churches that were purpose-driven. But now here was something new. Not a mission statement, not an outside slogan imposed on the community, but a framing story, a way of being, born from within the community, within their own stories and life together. Mike and Jim kept telling the congregation that they were a church that stood and fell, lived and died, on "Nothing can separate us from God's love."

Mike and Jim believe that this word—their watchword—differed from a mission statement or a framing slogan borrowed from a big church movement. But what made it so different?

Why did it feel like "Nothing can separate us from God's love" escaped being a trite catchphrase? After all, "Nothing can separate us from God's love" seems pretty generic and banal to most of us, probably to anyone not in the community.

What made it different is that everyone in the congregation (directly or indirectly) knew that the phrase had its origins in the direct act of God in the midst of despair. The word was wrapped inside a specific encounter with the living God.

The Jurgensons' shipwreck happened long before Mike had arrived at the church. The Jurgensons had raised a deaf son. The sign language between the boy and his parents bound them to each other. Yet the Jurgensons' love for the boy was met by the pain of cultural misunderstandings. It had been a challenge from the boy's earliest days. It was a challenge the Jurgensons faced together, and it had transformed them. Sign language was the language of love between them and their son. There was pain and struggle, but they had seen the boy into adulthood and were so proud of him. The life that lay ahead of him excited them. He had just married and launched into life, which brought them joy because of his joy.

But it wasn't to be. In his early twenties, a newlywed, their son fell ill and suddenly died. The grief was so acute it cut through both the Jurgensons, piercing to the place where soul meets body. It shook them to the core. Throughout their son's life, they'd reminded him over and over that "nothing can separate you from God's love." Not his difference, not his struggles, not the cruelty of others. Nothing. His parents and the God who is God loved him wildly and deeply. God had always been near their boy, present to him in tangible ways.

When illness took their son and death arrived, the word that was the boy's became the Jurgensons' word. The word encompassed so much. It was an artifact, even an altar like Jacob built at Bethel (Gen. 35), that testified that indeed God is in this hellish place. The watchword ministered directly to the Jurgensons, and they could do no other than give the word away. They felt compelled to invite a group of seventh graders to pick it up and see the world through it. They loved the seventh graders in the same language of love they shared with their son. The Jurgensons taught them sign language. It became the language of their prayers and reading of Scripture. The seventh graders were invited to look through the Jurgensons' son's own vision and see that "nothing can separate us from God's love." Everyone in the congregation—to one degree or another—had seen it. Many generations of middle schoolers had signed it with their hands and prayed it into their lives.

Everyone in the congregation knew that this word had weathered the harshest of realities. The word was like a worn piece of wood or leather, carried by the Jurgensons into the darkest and windiest of paths the soul can know. The word testified not to some religious platitudes or program of church growth, but to life that comes directly out of the pit of loss. These words were the revelation that comes out of a rupture so deep it shapes being. This word—nothing can separate us from God's love—had come miraculously bobbing to the surface with the force of mercy in the darkness of seas. The Jurgensons desperately grabbed hold and, clinging to the word, they couldn't help seeing everything in their lives through this word. It became for them the life raft that kept them from drowning.

When Mike and Jim moved the banner into the center of the congregation's worship, the entire congregation directly sensed, or knew, this depth. It was no catchword, no marketing hook, but a true description of dying and being embraced by the God who turns dying into life. Nothing separated the Jurgensons' son from the God who is God, from the God who acts, as the son and his parents faced his death. The Jurgensons were sure, as they faced the death of their son, that the watchword encompassed their own experience of the living God. Their deepest fear, their most bitter of sorrows, could not separate them from God's love. They discovered more assuredly than ever in this hell that God was with them. Not even the death of their most beloved son could separate them from the ministering love of Jesus. He was present, ever near to them.

How could they keep from telling a group of seventh graders to look for what they'd seen? Sunday school became a practice in watching with each other, entering the language of Scripture through sign language, as together they waited for God to come again and minister hope where there was none. The Jurgensons literally invited the seventh graders to crawl under the table and wait together, in silence, in darkness, for the God who brings the promises of life out of death.

Mike realized—and it became his form of leadership—that it was crucial to allow the Jurgensons' watchword to soak into every corner of the congregation. The job of the pastor—or the job of a board, session, or council—is to allow such a word to run like water into each crack. A church must say it again and again, not as some annoying team chant. Not as a catchphrase for T-shirts and beer cozies but as a confession of God's movement from death to life. The Jurgensons' "nothing can separate us from God's love" was a proclamation born from within a broken confession. It was Mike and Jim's sensitivity to the Holy Spirit to recognize this, to see the Jurgensons' word as an articulation of an encounter with the God who is God. It was Mike's humility and curiosity that led him to uncover and amplify this word—not necessarily the Jurgensons themselves. Mike wasn't concerned with making the Jurgensons into heroes. There was a paradox here, because it wasn't about them, but it had everything to do with them. It was about the God who moved directly in their lives. It was about their witness now coming to the entire congregation (and from the congregation to the world) of an encounter with the God who is God.

Mike's amplification of the Jurgensons' witness, solidified in a watchword, was proclamation. It was the proclamation that the God who is God was present to them all. Everyone in the congregation could know it. The congregation could see it if they remembered that "nothing can separate us from God's love." This "nothing can separate us from God's love" was the formative shorthand of the confession of God's direct work through the Spirit in their midst. Mike's leadership was to find and amplify the story of God's presence, not to venerate the Jurgensons (or redirect them into proper Sunday school formation). Mike's job, your job as a leadership team, was to amplify the good news of God's encounter encapsulated in a word of God's moving in the congregation.

For Prince of Peace Lutheran Church, the Jurgensons were inseparable from this reality, and yet it all pointed beyond them. Unlike a marketing pitch or campaign slogan, it was all done with humility and gratitude. How wildly wrong it would have been to use grieving parents to market the church! The Jurgensons carried their watchword like the faintest of candles flickering to survive against the winds of the darkest of storms—nothing, not even the death of their beloved boy, not even indescribable heartache, could separate them, or anyone at Prince of Peace, from the love of God. This was what Prince of Peace proclaimed to the world. The Jurgensons, their realness and their humanity, were a sign to the entire congregation of this truth.

No wonder the seventh graders crawled under the table with that old couple, hearing again and again the secret each week. A secret spilling directly from the Jurgensons' faces, weathered by the joy of their suffering met by the mercy of God. No wonder the seventh graders came to hear and see that this is a God who acts to embrace. And that this God, if searched for through the Jurgensons' word, could indeed encounter them. Through the Jurgensons, the seventh graders gave themselves over to the real possibility that this was true, that this was a promise they could shape their life around. Those seventh graders gave themselves over to it and remembered it every year when the Jurgensons called to sing happy birthday. They watched with the Jurgensons for this God who is God to move in their midst. Mike and Jim simply brought this to the whole congregation, naming it further, asking everyone to do like the seventh graders and crawl down into the darkness with this flickering light of the Jurgensons' watchword and wait for God.

It made them into a community.

Mike and Jim had been amplifying the Jurgensons' watchword, calling the congregation to wait with that watchword, when a young mother in their church came down with a strange sickness. For months, stretching into a year, there was no explanation for her illness. All treatments of the mysterious ailment did nothing. The young mother was in agony. After battling and battling, it became too much, and to everyone's shock, she took her own life. Her death turned the congregation upside down. Shock mixed with sorrow capsized them all. In the raging sea of hell, the whole congregation, confused and broken, grabbed for the Jurgensons' watchword. The funeral held it like a mantra, said as the deepest prayer, "*Nothing* can separate us from the love of God." The watchword had become inseparable from the life of the community, from the experience of the community's encounter with the God who arrives. They could only stop and wait, being together, meeting God and one another inside "nothing can separate us from the love of God." The watchword made them not only a community but a community standing before the living God who is God.

Their focus was never again on decline. Attention on the watchword eclipsed any sense of decline. It relativized, even minimized, the anxieties of decline. Such anxieties were placed far under the call to watch together for the living God. Mike and Jim now knew that when you get your whole church on the floor, knocked there by life, as you follow others into the roughest of seas to remember and wait for the God of Israel to arrive, it infuses the church with life.

Mike understands now that watchwords only come for a time. Now, twenty years later, the watchword that had its origins with the Jurgensons has passed away. Mike sees that because God moves in time, really acting in our lives, watchwords must come anew. He's seen a lot in his ministry. He's been at Prince of Peace for twenty-three years, ten of them as the senior pastor. Mike has pastored the church long enough to see a generation rise who does not know the Jurgensons, like the pharaoh who didn't know Joseph. Because watchwords are bound in a community's encounter with the living God, a watchword must be reborn in each new time. Like the Hebrew prophets, who come with a new word for a particular time, so a watchword will arrive, and after a time, disappear. A new watchword will need to lead the community, redirecting the community, moving the congregation into a new ministry in and for the world.

But how do you know when a watchword needs renewing? How do you find a new watchword? What Mike came to see is that you can't go looking for these words. These words must find you. But what you can do, Mike explains, is develop your ear. Mike believes you pastor and lead by ear. Too often, we think the best pastors (and boards, sessions, and councils) become the best because they have overwhelming capacities in skill, energy, creativity, and determination. That's not what Mike discovered. Rather, the most faithful pastors and boards, sessions, and councils listen by waiting. They have a developed ear. They listen to stories, watching for the ways the odd and beautiful forms of ministry take place. Mike explains that you must train your ear, much like a musician. Be patient enough to hear stories, to invite them to be told, to be curious about what stories might mean. You realize that what the church needs is not your creativity at all, but your listening and waiting.

What you're listening for, Mike explains, are those words that sound like a Bible verse. Mike pays particular attention to when people's narrative description of life and loss, of God's presence and absence in their lives, sounds like Scripture—that's what happened with the Jurgensons. Mike has now formed an entire staff and council with an ear. The staff leads the congregation by training the ear of the congregation with Scripture, inviting the people to share their stories, listening (and waiting) for the word that testifies to God working life out of death.

The watchword doesn't always come quickly. Mike explains that over his tenure at Prince of Peace, there have been spans where they were without a watchword. But eventually it comes—it always does. Inside one of those spans of having no watchword, Mike, the staff, and the council decided they'd commit to doing less. By praying, Mike learned that in such times—periods of discernment, in-between times—there was a great temptation to do more. To stop listening and waiting and push toward trying all sorts of new stuff. Mike felt like this wasn't right.

Therefore, in 2016, the congregation did less. The staff and council affirmed a fallow time necessary to let the soil rest. Inside this commitment to doing less, Mike discovered two things.

First, doing less actually meant more change. Before, the staff and council never had time to discuss or explore what was shaping their life together, particularly the ways the community could be more open to the leadership of others, inviting more voices to speak, calling others to give more attention to those voices, turning an ear to them. The staff and council always wanted to do that but never found the time. Now inside the waiting, inside the commitment to do less, they were making the most fundamental changes their congregation had seen in three or four decades. Doing less, paradoxically, provided the opportunity to make sweeping changes that were aimed not toward beating back decline but encountering God. Doing less shaped the community directly for a life together before a living God.

Second, Mike discovered that in doing less, in waiting, the new watchword came to the surface. When one watchword passes away and you need another, you need to do less and wait, listening for what sounds like Scripture. As 2016, the year of doing less, came to a close, a new watchword was birthed. It wasn't expected, but it arrived. The new watchword was "Never alone." It kept coming up in stories. Mike thought that it indeed sounded like Scripture, but also like a chant from the Liverpool Football Club. Mike also knew that the leader's job was not to control the watchword but to amplify it. It was clear that this was the new watchword; it captured stories within the congregation and without about encounters with God.

The "Never alone" watchword played its part for the next few years. The congregation centered its prayers on it and thought about the church's ministry in relation to it. But ultimately, they did not know why it was there. It was important in its own way, but Mike wasn't sure how God was using it. Then, in March 2020, the world shut down. COVID forced the entire congregation to be alone with their fears and isolation. "Never alone" became the word that framed the community's seeking of God inside the pandemic. It became the word that held them together. In the experience of loss, "Never alone" became the lens to look for the living God. With this watchword, the community began testifying to God's action in unique ways. The congregation, even over Zoom, held the watchword. "Never alone" framed their decision about returning to in-person worship and what shape that return would take. To this day, "Never alone" is shaping the congregation to wait for the God who is God, the God who promises that we are never alone.

# Notes

## Chapter 1 Why Your Church Has a Problem, but It Isn't What You Think

1. Let's get something out of the way for our non-American readers. One-half of the authors of this book is Canadian, and the other half wishes he were. We've lived and worked in different parts of the world. There are very real differences between places. Still, we think that our general analysis is true in most Western contexts even if the details are different. As we push into the book you will see that we focus on the congregation, a context that you know much better than us. So we hope you can put up with a few American-centered examples knowing that most of what we say applies to you, eh?

## Chapter 2 Busy People, Busy Church—A Killer Cocktail

1. The name came in the second century. We are not saying that the name caused the secular age, but it represents something key to the secular age. By putting the apostles as the main agents, the book focuses on human action, much like how the secular focus on the immanent frame excludes transcendent action.

## Chapter 3 Stop All the Having and Just Be

1. The stand-up routine referenced here comes from Aziz Ansari's Netflix show, *Aziz Ansari: Right Now* (2019).

2. All of the details about Mars Hill and Mark Driscoll are available online. Readers can profitably engage with the Mars Hill story through the Christianity Today podcast *The Rise and Fall of Mars Hill* at https://www.christianitytoday.com/ct/podcasts/rise-and-fall-of-mars-hill. Episode 7,

"State of Emergency," makes a number of references to the "Mars Hill bus" incident.

### Chapter 4  It's Time to Wait, but for What?

1. It isn't until Acts 13:9 that we find out that Saul is sometimes called Paul. People almost always call him Paul nowadays, and so will we.

### Chapter 5  Waiting Brings Life, Not a Slow Death

1. Dietrich Bonhoeffer, *Creation and Fall* (Minneapolis: Fortress, 1997), 31.

### Chapter 6  Forget the Mission Statement—Get a Watchword

1. This story and quotes about Martin Luther King Jr. come from Rufus Burrow Jr., *God and Human Dignity: The Personalism, Theology, and Ethics of Martin Luther King, Jr.* (Notre Dame, IN: University of Notre Dame Press, 2006), 105–7.

2. You can find out much more about PEEL at projectpeel.org.

3. The results of that show are at https://ashaandco.uk/news-articles/art-of-the-states.

4. Karl Barth, *Church Dogmatics* I/1, *The Doctrine of the Word of God*, trans. Geoffrey Bromiley, ed. T. F. Torrance (Edinburgh: T&T Clark, 1958), 60–61.